4.00

The Richest Man Who Ever Lived

"Truly amazing! Solomon gives us the master keys to success, wealth, and happiness. In this book, Steve Scott puts those keys in our hands and shows us how to use them. Whether you're just getting started in business or [are] the CEO of a Fortune 500 company, I believe these breakthrough strategies could propel you to levels of success and happiness you haven't yet imagined."
—DAVID NEELEMAN, CEO and chairman of the board of jetBlue Airways

"This is an exciting book. It will change your life to one of excellence and success. Though I, too, read a Proverbs chapter a day, I have never seen it all mapped out so clearly and practically. This will help so many—including me!"
—RUTH GRAHAM, author of *A Legacy of Love* and *A Legacy of Faith*

"Phenomenal! Steve Scott has 'cracked' the Solomon Code. He takes the inspired wisdom of Solomon and transforms it into simple yet powerful steps we can take to solve any problem and achieve true fulfillment and extraordinary success, at home and at work. Most important, he shows how anyone can partner with the ultimate mentor. This book will turn a purpose-driven life into a purpose-accomplished life!"
—CHUCK NORRIS, movie and television star

"Steven Scott knows God and he knows business. His new book, based upon the secrets of King Solomon's success, is dynamite! It will blow the dust off your heart and mind and stir you to action. *The Richest Man Who Ever Lived* is one of the best books I have ever read. Don't miss it."

—DR. JERRY FALWELL, founder and chancellor of Liberty University

"I've always loved the Proverbs, and Steve Scott converts Solomon's principles into specific, life-changing steps of action that anyone can take."

—DR. DAVID JEREMIAH, SR., pastor, author of *Sanctuary* and *Escape the Coming Night*

"Steve Scott's uncanny discernment enables us to understand Solomon's wisdom in a way that few of us ever have. More importantly, he shows us how to apply its life-transforming power to every important area of our lives—our marriages, our parenting, our jobs, and our faith."

—MICHAEL LANDON, JR., writer, director, producer

"For over thirty years Steven Scott has been 'hanging out' with the richest man who ever lived. In this book, you will get to hang out with Steven. It will enrich your life."

—GARY D. CHAPMAN, PHD, best-selling author of *The Five Love Languages* and *The Four Seasons of Marriage*

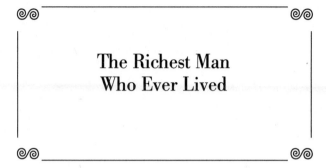

The Richest Man
Who Ever Lived

The Richest Man Who Ever Lived

King Solomon's Secrets to Success, Wealth, and Happiness

Steven K. Scott

FOREWORD BY
Dr. Gary Smalley

WATERBROOK
PRESS

THE RICHEST MAN WHO EVER LIVED
PUBLISHED BY WATERBROOK PRESS
12265 Oracle Boulevard, Suite 200
Colorado Springs, Colorado 80921

All Scripture quotations, unless otherwise indicated, are taken from the New American Standard Bible® (NASB). © Copyright The Lockman Foundation 1960, 1962, 1963, 1968, 1971, 1972, 1973, 1975, 1977, 1995. Used by permission. (www.Lockman.org). Scripture quotations marked (NIV) are taken from the Holy Bible, New International Version®. NIV®. Copyright © 1973, 1978, 1984 by International Bible Society. Used by permission of Zondervan Publishing House. All rights reserved. Scripture quotations marked (KJV) are taken from the King James Version. Scripture quotations marked (NKJV) are taken from the New King James Version®. Copyright © 1982 by Thomas Nelson Inc. used by permission. All rights reserved.

Italicized words in Scripture quotations reflect the author's emphasis.

Proprietary ISBN 9780385365895

Published in the United States by WaterBrook Multnomah, an imprint of the Crown Publishing Group, a division of Penguin Random House LLC, New York.

WATERBROOK and its deer colophon are registered trademarks of Penguin Random House LLC.

Printed in the United States of America

Cover Illustration © Giraudon/Art Resource, NY
Cover Design by T. Oliver Peabody

2017

10 9 8 7 6 5 4 3 2 1

SPECIAL SALES
Most WaterBrook books are available in special quantity discounts when purchased in bulk by corporations, organizations and special interest groups. Custom imprinting or excerpting can also be done to fit special needs. For information, please e-mail SpecialMarkets@WaterBrookMultnomah.com or call 1-800-603-7051.

Dedicated to:

My Proverbs 31-wife, Shannon Lory Scott;
and Bob Marsh, Gary Smalley, and Jim Shaughnessy.
Your lives have provided me with a wonderful,
day-by-day, lifetime demonstration of the wisdom and
power of King Solomon's Proverbs.

My children, Carol, Mark, Zach, Devin, Ryan,
Sean, and Hallie Rose;
and my grandchildren, Madelyn, Julia, and Gracie.
May the wisdom of Proverbs fill your lives with
never-ending joy, purpose, and fulfillment.

My loving sister, Sandy; her wise husband,
Dr. David Heinze; and
my awesome niece & nephews, Bethany, Tim,
Nathan, and Christian.

Two of the best lifetime friends a man could ever have,
Tom & Marlene Delnoce

*Tremendous thanks to my brilliant editor,
Roger Scholl, Senior Editor, Doubleday.
You are the best I've ever worked with …
by a million miles!*

*My deep appreciation and thanks to my wonderful
literary agents, Michael Broussard and Jan Miller.
Thanks for your never-ending encouragement and
belief in the importance of this book.*

Contents

— ◉◉ —

Foreword by Dr. Gary Smalley

In 1974, as I was spending the night at Steve Scott's small home in Phoenix, Arizona, he told me of his career difficulties. Steve was a little discouraged at the time. He had just lost his sixth job since graduating from college four years earlier. It seemed to him that no matter how hard he tried, he couldn't keep a job for more than a few months. He had even tried starting his own business a couple of times, but both had quickly failed. He wanted to know if I could offer him any suggestions. I asked him to let me think about it overnight, and we could resume our talk in the morning. After praying about it, I had an idea. I gave him a challenge as we ate breakfast. I asked Steve, "How would you like to become smarter than all of your bosses?"

He replied, somewhat sarcastically, "Yeah, right."

"No," I told him. "I can promise that if you'll just do one

thing, within two years you'll be smarter than all of your future bosses. And I'll bet you'll be a millionaire within five years."

He thought I was nuts. Then he asked what he would need to do. Here's what I told him: "There are thirty-one days in the month, and there are thirty-one chapters in the biblical Book of Proverbs. Every day, at the start of each day, read the chapter in Proverbs that corresponds to that particular date. Read two chapters on the last day of months that have only thirty days. Do that every day, month after month, and I guarantee that within two years you'll be smarter than all of your bosses. Do it for five years, and I'll bet you become a millionaire." I told him to read it with a pen and paper at hand so he could make notes about the knowledge and wisdom he would be learning. I believed that the wisdom Steve would learn from Proverbs would change his life. What I didn't know was that he would then use his newly acquired wisdom to change mine.

Steve took up my challenge and began reading a chapter of Proverbs every day. Within two years, he had followed Solomon's advice to find a business partner, and together they launched a start-up marketing company. Within a few months, their company was making a million dollars a week. Steve did become a multimillionaire in fairly short order, but that's *not* the end of the story.

Two years after he and his partner started their business, he called and asked me if I'd like to write a couple of books on marriage. I had never written a book and had been praying for ten years for the opportunity to write a book on marriage.

Now here was Steve asking me to write two—one for men and one for women. Together we wrote my first two books in near-miraculous time, two months. Steve wrote and produced a commercial with Pat and Shirley Boone talking about the two books, and as a result, *If Only He Knew* and *For Better or for Best* became international bestsellers, changing the lives of millions of families. But that still isn't the end of the story. Years later, Steve asked me if I'd like to create a video series to help millions more. Together we produced *Hidden Keys to Loving Relationships*. Steve then wrote and produced infomercials featuring John Tesh and Connie Sellecca to put those videos into millions of homes and tens of thousands of church libraries. It is safe to say that without the launching of my first two books and the *Hidden Keys* video series, there would be no Smalley Relationship Center today.

Steve Scott has not only helped me achieve my dreams— for more than thirty years, he has been one of my closest friends. The wisdom he received from the Book of Proverbs has changed his life, my life, and the lives of millions who have benefited from our life's work. When I first heard his CD series *Lessons from the Richest Man Who Ever Lived,* I was blown away by its content. I ordered forty sets, one for each member of my family and every employee on our staff. For two years, Steve and I have talked about the need to put this material into print. I am thrilled that the world is about to become acquainted with the incomparable wisdom and incredibly practical insights, advice, and warnings of Solomon. As you read this book, Steve will take Solomon's teachings and deliver them with a life-changing power and practical simplicity that I believe can bring about dramatic changes in your life. I hope that this is only the first of many books that Steve will write on the Proverbs that have so radically changed his life and mine.

The Richest Man
Who Ever Lived

How the Richest Man Who Ever Lived Can Make You Happier, More Successful, and Wealthier

Imagine going from a below-average wage to a personal income of more than $600,000 per *month!* Imagine losing nine jobs in your first six years after college, and then, on your tenth job, building more than a dozen multimillion-dollar businesses from scratch, achieving sales of billions of dollars. Imagine doing all of this by following specific steps taught by Solomon in the Old Testament Book of Proverbs. In a nutshell, that is my personal story. Now think about it:

Before: Earned less than half of the income of the average American wage earner.

After: Income rose from $18,000 per year to more than $7 million.

Before: Diagnosed a hopeless corporate failure with a success rate of 0 percent.

After: A twenty-nine-year career success rate of over 60

percent in an industry where the average success rate is under 1 percent.

And just as convincing to me is what happened when I acted *contrary* to Solomon's advice. On three occasions, I violated three of his warnings and lost millions of dollars through bad investment decisions. Had I followed Solomon's advice, I would not have lost a penny. I ignored his advice on relationships and watched one of the happiest marriages in America fall apart. Then, following Solomon's advice on relationships, my marriage was restored and today is happier than ever!

If following Solomon's advice had worked only a few times in the course of my life, we could call it coincidence. If ignoring his advice and warnings had resulted in a few minor setbacks, we could call it chance. But when following his advice has created such significant personal, business, and financial success year after year for me and for countless others, and failing to heed his warnings has caused heartbreaking personal and financial disasters, even the heartiest skeptic must admit what wise men and kings and queens the world over once acknowledged—that Solomon was the wisest man who ever lived.

Just as there are physical laws that govern the physical universe, Solomon reveals "laws of living" that invisibly govern all aspects of life.

Every time you step on board an airliner, the physical laws of gravity and aerodynamics govern your ultimate destiny. If your pilot and the airplane operate in accordance with those laws, you will safely arrive at your destination. If for any reason whatsoever they do not operate in accordance with those laws, you will return to the ground, one way or another. It doesn't matter how you feel about these laws, whether you love them or hate them, whether you choose to ignore them or not; they *still* exist and they *will* govern your flight. Fortunately, pilots, aeronautical engineers, and aircraft designers fully understand these laws, and thus they are able to use them to great advantage. They are able to build and fly aircraft that move us quickly, safely, and comfortably to our destinations. If they were ignorant of these laws, no airplanes would be able to fly.

Just as there are physical laws that govern the universe, there are laws of living that are just as sure and true. It doesn't matter if you love them or hate them, they *still* exist, and they *will* govern your life. Solomon reveals these laws in the biblical Book of Proverbs, and more important, shows us how to use them to our advantage. The laws of gravity and aerodynamics have always existed, but until they were learned and understood, they kept the entire human race on the ground; once they were discovered, they became the very basis for achieving human flight.

The laws of living are as old as human life itself. Being ignorant of them only restricts your ability to achieve genuine happiness, fulfillment, purpose, and success. Many people act in accordance with some of these laws coincidentally, without knowing or understanding them, and they gain a level of success or happiness by doing so. But more often than not, ignorance of these laws creates insurmountable barriers to sustained success and fulfillment. On the other hand, those who learn these laws and how to use them in their flight through life will achieve a level of purpose, success, and happiness that others can only dream of. The purpose-*driven* life will become the purpose-*accomplished* life.

◎◎ The Prayer of Solomon

Solomon was born around 974 B.C. and was installed as King of Israel by his father, David, shortly before David died. Solomon was twelve years old. Solomon was terrified of ruling Israel, afraid that he didn't have the wisdom to do so. According to the Old Testament, God appeared to Solomon and asked him what he wanted. Solomon answered, asking only for wisdom and knowledge so that he could rightly judge the great people of Israel (I Kings 3:9; II Chronicles 1:10). God then told Solomon that because he had not asked for riches, wealth, honor, the life of his enemies, nor a longer life for himself, He would give Solomon more wisdom, knowledge, riches, wealth, and honor than any king before him or any king that would come after him. What was promised was delivered. Solomon's wisdom, success, and wealth increased beyond imagination. In terms of wealth, some have suggested that in today's dollars, he may well have been a "trillionaire." In addition to his gold reserves worth hundreds of billions of dollars in today's market, he owned 4,000 stalls for his horses and chariots, and kept 12,000 horsemen on his payroll. Rulers of nations throughout the world sought his advice, and paid dearly for it. However, by the middle of his life, he began to violate the laws of living, its principles and strategies that he so wisely articulated in the Book of Proverbs; as he did, his success and happiness vaporized. Fortunately for us, he recorded many of his laws for living in the Book of Proverbs.

⊚⊚ Cracking the Solomon Code

Although each Proverb provides an obvious insight, often the real treasure of a Proverb is buried deep beneath its surface. Solomon implores us in chapter 2, verse 4, to search for wisdom and knowledge as we would search for silver or buried treasure. To do this, we must often look deeper beneath the surface, at the background of the Proverb, its context, and even nuances of the Hebrew words that make up the original text of Proverbs. In many cases, we can find added treasure by looking at the converse meaning of a Proverb. And last, but not least, we must look at the broader spirit of the Proverb and not just the narrow meaning of the literal statement. As we do this, we not only discover Solomon's laws for living, we find the silver and buried treasure he talked about—treasure that will last beyond our lifetime.

I'm not the only person who has achieved his impossible dreams by following Solomon's strategies. I love reading biographies of those who have achieved extraordinary accomplishments, both in modern times and throughout history. As I have studied their lives, I have discovered that their successes, too, were realized by actions and attitudes that reflected Solomon's teachings, even though some may have never read his writings. George Washington, Thomas Jefferson, Abraham Lincoln, Henry Ford, and Thomas Edison were all readers of Proverbs in their youth. But even in looking at the lives of modern icons such as Bill Gates, Sam Walton, Helen Keller, Steven Spielberg, and Oprah Winfrey, we see that they have achieved their impossible dreams by doing the very things that Solomon advises each of us to do. I've also seen disasters befall men, companies, and nations when they acted contrary to Solomon's admonitions. Adolf Hitler was able to bewitch an entire nation because they ignored Solomon's warnings. America was caught off guard at Pearl Harbor. Recently, the executives of America's seventh-largest corporation drove it into the largest corporate bankruptcy in American history. All of these events were brought about by violating a handful of Solomon's admonitions.

What Can Solomon's Wisdom Do for You?

So what can Solomon's insights and teachings do for your career, your relationships, and your personal life? No matter what you *think* they can do, they can do infinitely more. Here are just a few of the rewards Solomon says you can look forward to when you follow his advice.

The Benefits of Solomon's Strategies
- Knowledge
- Discretion

- Good judgment
- Preservation and protection
- Success
- Better health
- Longer life
- Honor
- Financial abundance
- Favor of those in authority
- Commendation and promotions
- Financial independence
- Confidence
- Strength of character
- Courage
- Extraordinary achievement
- Personal fulfillment
- Great relationships
- A truly meaningful life
- Love and admiration of others
- Understanding
- True wisdom

Solomon gives us powerful strategies and life-changing tactics for achieving extraordinary outcomes.

Don't make the mistake of thinking that what you're about to read is simply a collection of general principles and poetic platitudes. Solomon was far too wise to waste his time and yours with such meaningless generalities. His writings provide precise steps that can be taken in your personal and professional life to produce astounding results. In this book, I focus on the strategies and steps articulated in the biblical Book of Proverbs that I have applied to the business, personal, and financial areas of my own life. After we examine Solomon's advice in each chapter, I will then offer some simple techniques that I have used to implement his advice in my daily life.

At the conclusion of each chapter, I've added a section called "Knowledge to Wisdom," with specific exercises to enable you to apply Solomon's advice in a practical and powerful way. Do this, and you will begin to experience a greater level of success and personal fulfillment than you have ever imagined. No matter how successful you may be right now, your future is about to get a whole lot better. Let the adventure begin!

CHAPTER 2

The Key to Winning Every Race

Do you see a man diligent in his business?
He shall stand before kings.

—PROVERBS 22:29

Become the One in a Thousand Who Achieves Incredible Outcomes

In any endeavor we undertake, or any goal we pursue, we can experience outcomes that are incredible, great, good, okay, poor, terrible, or catastrophic. In my fifty-plus years, I have experienced all of these outcomes personally, professionally, and financially. Studying the lives of many of history's most successful people, I discovered that they, too, have experienced the gamut of these outcomes in one or more areas of their lives. But in the areas of their greatest achievements, without exception, they have achieved *incredible* outcomes. And every one of them achieved their incredible outcomes because they learned and utilized one simple, yet incredibly powerful, skill. This skill was their key to achieving their impossible dreams. George Washington, Thomas

Jefferson, Benjamin Franklin, Thomas Edison, Clara Barton, John D. Rockefeller, Henry Ford, Sam Walton, Walt Disney, Bill Gates, Oprah Winfrey, and Steven Spielberg are just a few of the people who have used it. The fact is, whenever it is used, it ultimately produces incredible outcomes. Moreover, incredible outcomes are almost never achieved without it.

Unfortunately, less than one in a thousand people fully utilize it. The good news is that it is a skill that can be easily learned. And it can be used by anyone, regardless of their background, education, or IQ.

I'm talking about the skill of *diligence*. Most people think they understand what diligence means, but nothing could be further from the truth. When Solomon talks about diligence, he's talking about a trait that is as rare as a ten-carat diamond. The reason it's so rare is that true diligence runs contrary to human nature.

We all have traits that are part of the human condition. These traits produce our natural drives, inclinations, strengths, and weaknesses. Diligence, however, is not one of them. In fact, the trait common to all humans is our desire or drive for instant gratification. We want as much as we can get, as fast as we can get it, with as little effort as possible. *That* is our nature. We all have a natural inclination to follow the path of least resistance. Fortunately, despite our natural inclination, we can *choose* to follow a path of greater resistance and become diligent in the pursuit of any endeavor, project, or goal. And if you develop the kind of diligence that Solomon refers to, you can achieve incredible outcomes in any important area of your life.

◉◉ Solomon's Concept of Diligence (It's Not What You Think)

My computer dictionary describes diligence as "a persistent and hard-working effort in doing something." I love the word "persistent"; persistence is certainly a part of diligence. "Hard-working," on the other hand, is not the most accurate term to use when trying to understand Solomon's meaning. I'd prefer to use the phrase "smart-working." If I need to cut down a tree and try to cut it down with a hammer, that would be hard-working, but it certainly would not be diligent. It could take me hours, even days, to chop down a tree with a hammer. On the other hand, if I use a chain saw I might cut that same tree down in minutes. I would not be working nearly as hard, but I'd be working a lot smarter. My computer software lists the following words as synonyms of diligence: meticulousness, conscientiousness, thoroughness, and carefulness. Although all of these qualities are important aspects of diligence, they do not fully convey Solomon's meaning.

To fully understand what Solomon meant by the word "diligent," we need to add those qualities to Solomon's words found in Proverbs 20:11: "Even a child is known by his doings, whether his work be *pure and whether it be right.*" The key words here are "pure" and "right." Solomon uses the word "pure" not just in the sense of a moral or ethical value, but rather about work in its purest form. It's more akin to a mining term than an ethical term. Solomon's mines represented a tremendous portion of his wealth; he often used mining terms in his writings. And if you're mining for gold, what do you do? You dig a lot of dirt, you find a big rock, and you take that big rock and subject it to a tremendous amount of heat. This melts all of the impurities. What's left behind is pure gold. That is the "pure" side of diligence. It's getting down to investing one's days, hours, and minutes in that which brings a pure return on the time and effort invested.

The other side of diligence is the "right" side. It's not just about working at something with persistence and by working smart. It's about doing it *right*—expeditiously, efficiently, and effectively. In other words, doing it on time to the highest standards possible, regardless of what is demanded or expected. It means bringing creativity, persistence, and even other people and outside resources into the effort to achieve an extraordinary outcome.

DILIGENCE is a learnable skill that combines: *creative persistence,* a *smart-working* effort *rightly planned* and *rightly performed* in a *timely, efficient,* and *effective* manner to attain a result that is *pure* and of the highest quality of *excellence*.

Now, before you back away and say, "That's just not me. I'm not a creative or persistent kind of person," let me tell you, you can be. All you need to do is follow Solomon's recipe for developing the skill of diligence. He understood that anyone could develop this skill. Remember, he said, "Even a *child* . . ." And once we've mastered the art of diligence, we can use it in any important area of our lives, in any endeavor or pursuit, to achieve *incredible* outcomes. We can use it to turn poor marriages into great marriages; good careers into incredible careers; and a failing business into a successful one.

Sound complicated? That's because true diligence involves many qualities. That is why true diligence is so rare. Perhaps it might be more easily understood by a simple illustration.

My freshman year of college, I was made a platoon commander in ROTC. The other thirty-nine platoon commanders were juniors and seniors. The major ROTC event of the year was the annual drill competition among the forty platoons. Prior to the competition, one officer thought his platoon would win hands down. He thought he and his platoon had been diligent all year in their weekly 7:00 A.M. drill sessions. What he didn't know was that my platoon showed up every week at 6:00 A.M. (voluntarily) and practiced for two hours instead of one. He didn't realize that I had taught my platoon complex drill-team maneuvers during the hour each week that we alone occupied the drill field. Every one of the thirty cadets in my platoon worked diligently to master the maneuvers.

By the time the competition rolled around, we had practiced twice as many hours and learned far more complex routines. In relation to the other platoons, we had been *truly* diligent, while the others only thought they were being diligent. The result was an "incredible outcome." My platoon won the event, scoring 287 points out of a possible 300. The favored platoon placed second, scoring only 168 points. I was the only freshman to command a platoon in the history of

ROTC at Arizona State University to win the annual drill competition. I was named Cadet of the Year, given a ninety-minute ride in a supersonic fighter, and offered an Air Force flight scholarship to pay for the remaining three years of my college education. In all fairness, however, we *all* won it—my entire platoon. And we did it, not because we were smarter or better educated, but because we were truly diligent.

◎◎ The Rewards of Becoming Truly Diligent

It is human nature to follow the path of least resistance. Solomon understood that we need to be motivated to choose diligence over our natural inclination to "go with the flow." And what is that motivation? Being truly diligent, he tells us, brings us priceless rewards, while a lack of diligence can produce devastating consequences. Here are some of the rewards he promises.

You will gain sure advantage.

In any endeavor, would you rather pursue it having a strong and unshakable advantage, or having a lasting handicap? Solomon assures us that those who are truly diligent will gain an insurmountable advantage over those who are not. He says, "The plans of the diligent lead surely to advantage" (Proverbs 21:5). Whether we're competing against companies, individuals, circumstances, or simply time, diligence will give us a unique advantage, one that will result in greater productivity, achievement, wealth, and fulfillment.

You will be in control of the situation, rather than have the situation control you.

Would you prefer to have your life controlled by your boss and other people, or would you rather control your own life? Solomon says, "The hand of the diligent will rule, but the slack hand will be put to forced labor" (Proverbs 12:24). Those who are truly diligent not only control their own destiny, but enhance the achievements of those around them as well.

You will experience true fulfillment.

The vast majority of people are in a perpetual state of hunger. Not for food, at least in America, but for things. Americans today have more debt and lower savings than any generation in our nation's history. No matter what we have, it seems as if it is never enough. Contentment and true fulfillment seem to be as rare as a winning lottery ticket. In contrast, Solomon tells us, "The soul of the diligent is made fat" (Proverbs 13:4). When using the word "soul," Solomon is referring to a man or woman's innermost being, their very core, the seat of their personality and emotions. Imagine being so contented and fulfilled that you crave nothing. That's the kind of fulfillment that is promised to the diligent.

You will attain the respect and admiration of those in authority.

While others fight to be noticed, the diligent are sought out by people in positions of authority or prominence. That is what Solomon means when he says that the person who is diligent in their business "shall stand before kings" (Proverbs 22:29). Their achievements become bright stars that give off so much light that they draw the attention of all around them.

Your needs will be satisfied.

Those who work diligently in their field of expertise will achieve enough material success to satisfy their needs. In Proverbs 28:19, Solomon writes, "He that tills his land shall be satisfied with bread, but he that follows vain persons is void of understanding." Here he also warns that if you stray from your field of endeavors to follow vain people or their advice, you will lose the path to understanding. Translation: Don't be fooled by people who look successful on the surface and offer "get-rich-quick schemes" that sound too good to be true. They are. When you encounter such people, run away.

You will experience ever-increasing success.

Solomon assures us that those who diligently labor will experience success and wealth that continually grow, but money that comes to us easily, without significant effort, will nearly always be lost. He says, "Wealth gotten by vanity shall be diminished but he that gathers by labor shall increase" (Proverbs 13:11). As hard as it is to believe, most lottery winners lose all of their winnings in a relatively short amount of time. And even gamblers who are lucky enough to win big eventually lose their winnings and end up in debt. The casinos in Las Vegas don't offer free palatial hotel suites to high rollers out of the goodness of their heart. They do it because they know that no matter how much a high roller wins, he will ultimately lose a lot more.

Your efforts will be profitable.

Solomon promises that ALL diligent labor results in a profit—one that is measured by the successful achievement of your goals, and the financial reward you receive for achieving those goals. In Proverbs 14:23, he says, "In all labor there is profit, but mere talk leads only to poverty." Apply that labor to your marriage or your parenting efforts, and your profit will be measured by the amount of fulfillment you and your family gain. Mere talk, on the other hand, Solomon warns, is cheap and easy, and leads only to poverty. Diligent labor is demanding. It requires vision, creativity, commitment, and effective partnering. Essentially, Solomon is telling us that if you are not profitable in your career, or if your marriage isn't as fulfilling as you wish, you are probably not working diligently enough. Applying diligence to any area of our lives always brings profitable results.

◉ The Consequences of Not Being Diligent

Our greatest motivations in life are *the desire for gain* and *the fear of loss*. Solomon tries to motivate us with both. If his seven rewards don't provide the motivation you need to pursue diligence, perhaps the consequences of not being diligent will spur you on.

You will always be at an insurmountable disadvantage.

The diligent take all the time they need to plan and prepare, so that they can perform with excellence. Those who aren't diligent fail to take the time they need to plan, prepare, or perform. They tend to "shoot from the hip," and their haste ultimately results in failure. Solomon says, "The plans of the diligent lead surely to advantage. But everyone who is hasty [comes] surely to poverty" (Proverbs 21:5).

I have lost my life savings five times, and in each instance I acted with haste—I was anything but diligent. The first two times, my losses came to $20,000 and $120,000, respectively. The next three times, the amounts were much greater, in the millions of dollars. Similarly, my daughter lost her savings when she acted hastily without seeking counsel from me or others. Had either of us acted with diligence rather than in haste, she would still have a nice savings account, and I would have millions of dollars more in my financial portfolio.

You will be ruled.

No one likes living their life out of control. We hate being overly controlled by others. Yet Solomon warns, "The hand of the diligent will rule, but the slack hand will be put to forced labor" (Proverbs 12:24). Who decides how you spend your days? How much money you'll be paid? Whether or not you'll be promoted, demoted, or even let go? Even with those who own their own businesses, if they are not diligent, they are controlled by their customers or their competition.

You will crave, but will find little solace.

While those who are diligent see their deepest desires satisfied and enjoy a profound sense of fulfillment, those who lack diligence are subjected to endless cravings that can never be fulfilled. In Proverbs 13:4, Solomon not only tells us that the soul of the diligent will be made fat, he warns, "The soul of the sluggard craves, but he gets nothing." Sadly, for those who lack diligence, their lives are defined by desire rather than fulfillment.

You will lack understanding.

Today, the television airwaves are filled with people who promise wealth without work. You can buy real estate with no money down, make hundreds of thousands of dollars in stock trading even if you have no money in savings, and on and on. Solomon cautions that those who chase after quick-buck artists and their get-rich-quick schemes demonstrate only their ignorance. "He that tills his land shall be satisfied with bread, but he that follows vain persons is void of understanding" (Proverbs 28:19).

Your wealth and security will dissipate.

> **Wealth gotten by vanity shall be diminished, but he that gathers by labor shall increase.**   —*Proverbs 13:11*

Solomon contrasts the two ways people gain wealth: those who gain it through their diligent efforts and those who gain it without working for it. In Proverbs 13:11, he warns that those who gain their wealth through vain pursuits will see that wealth decrease and ultimately disappear.

Your efforts will come to nothing.

Those who diligently labor work heartily, while others are constantly talking about what they will do *someday*. Talk is cheap. It requires no effort. Diligent labor requires a great deal of effort. But while the diligent is profiting from his labors, the talker is merely wasting his—and others'—time. That's why Solomon tells us in Proverbs 14:23 that "mere talk leads only to poverty."

How can you bring true diligence into every area of your life?

Solomon gives us four steps that anyone can use to make diligence a part of his or her daily life. However, there's one giant roadblock. It's a roadblock that we will encounter nearly every day. I'm speaking of our inherent tendency to take the path of least resistance, our innate laziness.

Few of us view ourselves as lazy. But the truth is, we all have the *seeds* of laziness within our nature. And if they are not dealt with, they will grow into a field that will undermine one or more aspects of our lives. Left unattended, they can choke the potential from our lives. Often, we confront the seeds of laziness in one area of life, such as our job or career, and leave them unattended in other areas, such as our marriages or our relationships with our children. I have known men who have made great fortunes in their professional lives while their marriages end in divorce. It doesn't have to be this way. Solomon shows us how to deal with these seeds, wherever they lie, and replace them with the seeds of diligence.

๑๑ Recognizing the Root Causes of Laziness

There are four root causes of laziness, according to Solomon: self-centeredness, conceit (arrogance), ignorance, and irresponsibility. (He often combines these last two into the single category he calls foolishness.) To effectively deal with laziness, we have to deal with its root causes.

Self-Centeredness

Every man's way is right in his own eyes . . .

—*Proverbs 21:2*

We naturally see things first from our own point of view. If we don't choose to shift our focus to the interests and well-being of others, we will simply act in a manner that is most quickly gratifying to our ego and desires. We become blind to the impact on our future, or upon the lives of others. Solomon suggests we ask ourselves what course of action we could take that would be in the *best* interest of *all* who are affected.

Conceit (Arrogance)

The sluggard is wiser in his own conceit than seven men that can render a reason . . .   —*Proverbs 26:16*

Because we often think we're smarter than those around us, we act without seeking the advice or counsel of others. It's much easier to act first and seek advice later. And since we think we know more than others anyway, we simply take the action that we want to take. We simply need to accept that there are others who are as smart and wise as we are, if not more so, and seek their counsel before making major decisions and acting upon them. Those who are truly diligent seek out the advice of several wise counselors *before* embarking on any important course of action.

Ignorance and Irresponsibility (Foolishness)

I went by the field of the slothful, and by the vineyard of the man void of understanding; And, lo, it was all grown over with thorns, and nettles had covered the face thereof, and the stone wall thereof was broken down.   —Proverbs 24:30–31

The last cause of laziness is ignorance and irresponsibility, or what Solomon calls foolishness. Often it results from our ignorance of the long-term consequences of our actions. It's *easier* to act out of ignorance than it is to become educated. To educate ourselves takes time and effort. Remaining ignorant and following the path of least resistance is easy. However, the consequences of this kind of foolishness can be devastating. Even worse is irresponsibility—knowing what you should do, and choosing *not* to do it.

Laziness Results in More Laziness.

The sluggard will not plow by reason of the cold; therefore shall he beg in harvest, and have nothing.   —Proverbs 20:4

Laziness can spread into other areas of your life, as well. The more often you give in to your natural inclination toward instant gratification, the stronger that inclination will become, until it becomes a habit.

Laziness creates a painful barrier to personal achievement. In Proverbs 15:19, Solomon says, "The way of the slothful man is as an hedge of thorns." When I was a child, my next-door neighbor's backyard was surrounded by a deep hedge with red berries and big thorns. We dreaded those occasions when my friends and I would accidentally throw a baseball or football into Mr. Fouts's backyard. One of us would have to fight our way through the thornbushes to retrieve the ball. And whoever did the retrieving had the bloody scratches to show for it. In the eyes of Solomon, laziness creates this same kind of barrier to personal success. Few are able or willing to cross over.

ᐒ Solomon's Steps to Bring Diligence into Your Life

So how do we bring Solomon's concept of diligence into our lives? Being truly diligent takes time and requires making a habit of using diligence daily in the important areas of life. The good news is, you don't have to wait years, months, or even days to start applying diligence to your endeavors. Solomon gives us four steps we can use quickly to begin to bring diligence into our jobs, our careers, our marriages, our parenting, even the spiritual arena of our lives.

Step #1—Wake Up to Reality

"How long will you lie there," he asks. "When will you get up from your sleep? . . . poverty will come on you like a bandit and scarcity like an armed man."
—Proverbs 6:9–11

We think that we have more time than we really do to achieve our personal and professional goals. So we procrastinate doing what we know we should do. For example, almost 80 percent of Americans are now overweight. Nearly every one of them thinks they will start losing weight next week, next month, or next year. They plan on eating better, exercising more, and taking better care of themselves. But year after year, they don't quite get around to it. Getting into better shape remains only a dream for them, because they are asleep to their own reality. Similarly, husbands and wives and moms and dads plan to make their marriages and families better . . . later! Solomon says, WAKE UP and STOP PROCRASTINATING!

Don't be asleep to the realities around you. Solomon asks us to wake up to the real world, with its constraints, its demands, and its opportunities. The clock is constantly ticking, and every day that slips away is a day that can never be retrieved. And every day that passes brings us one day closer to the end of our limited time on earth. Wake up and bring diligence into your life now. Your opportunities will be multiplied! Take responsibility for your life, your attitudes, your values, and how you spend your time.

Step #2—Define Your Visions

Solomon wrote in Proverbs 28:19, "Without a vision, the people perish." Said another way, where we have no vision, we lose our direction, our motivation, our joy, our passion, our energy, our creativity, and our commitment. Fortunately, the converse of this proverb is also true. Whenever you introduce a true vision into any area of your life, you gain new energy. You will discover direction, motivation, joy, passion, energy, creativity, and commitment. Defining a vision is an essential component of diligence. In fact, it's impossible to be truly diligent if you don't have a clear vision of what you want to achieve. Bringing diligence into your life is the single most important step you can take. In Proverbs 6:6, Solomon tells those who lack diligence to look closely at the ant. The ant "has no commander, no overseer or ruler, yet it stores its provisions in summer and gathers its food at harvest." In other words, the ant is so mission oriented that even without supervision or direction, it does exactly what it needs to do for its benefit and the benefit of the entire colony. When you gain a clear vision of what you want to do, and when you have a detailed plan to accomplish that vision, like Solomon's ant, you will take the initiative and gain the diligence to accomplish it.

Step #3—Effectively Partner

> **Plans fail for lack of counsel, but with many advisers they succeed.**   **—Proverbs 15:22**

In any worthwhile endeavor, it's impossible to be diligent without seeking outside counsel and effectively partnering. We all know a little; no one knows a lot. Most of us are deeply knowledgeable in only a few things, and we're totally ignorant and incapable in millions of other things. Yet true diligence demands excellence in every step we take. The only possible way to achieve excellence in the areas in which we lack the necessary talent or know-how is to seek out counsel and/or effectively partner. When I talk about partnering, I'm referring to asking the help of advisers, counselors, mentors, and anyone else who can provide us with the knowledge and skills we need to achieve excellence in fulfilling our vision.

Throughout history, no one has achieved any worthwhile goal, significant project, or impossible dream without effectively partnering and seeking outside counsel. If the most successful people in history have needed the help of counselors and partners, why would you think that you can accomplish anything worthwhile without such aid? The fact is, none of us can. The truly diligent do not seek counsel simply when an endeavor is in trouble; rather, they seek counsel from the very beginning, *before* they begin an effort. This greatly reduces the risk of failure and significantly increases one's probability of success.

Step #4—Pursue Wisdom; Build Your Life Upon It

How much better it is to get wisdom than gold! And to get understanding is to be chosen above silver.
—*Proverbs 16:16*

The final component critical to becoming a diligent person is to pursue wisdom and build your life upon its foundation. Solomon tells us to seek wisdom as if it were a hidden treasure. True wisdom is rarely found lying on the ground in plain view. Rather, it's a treasure that must be searched out, and those seeking it must often dig beneath the surface. But it's not a difficult pursuit. It's fun to search for buried treasure, and it's wonderfully rewarding to find it. As you will see in the last chapter of this book, the rewards of gaining true wisdom are literally beyond your imagination.

It's impossible to be diligent in any endeavor without first gaining a clear and precise vision for what you want to achieve. In the next chapter you will discover how to develop an empowering vision for each important endeavor, project, and priority in your life.

Knowledge to Wisdom

Are you diligent in your job? Your marriage? Your parenting? Your career? Use this checklist to measure your level of diligence in any important area of your life. This checklist will help you determine when and where you're lacking in diligence. The skills you're going to learn in the next two chapters will help you to bring diligence to any endeavor you pursue.

DILIGENCE CHECKLIST

DO YOU:

___ 1. Have a clear and precise vision for what you want to achieve?

___ 2. Creatively persist through disappointments and failures?

___ 3. Work smart?

___ 4. "Rightly" plan?

___ 5. "Rightly" perform?

___ 6. Work expeditiously (with target dates)?

___ 7. Work efficiently?

___ 8. Work effectively (achieving effective results)?

___ 9. Produce a result that reflects a quality outcome?

___ 10. Attain true excellence?

CHAPTER 3

The Activity That Creates Extraordinary Success

Where there is no vision, the people perish.

—PROVERBS 29:18

I was recently given a tour of one of the Navy's frontline nuclear aircraft carriers, the USS *John C. Stennis.* The moment I stepped on board, I was amazed by its massive size. It's longer than three football fields, weighs nearly 200 million pounds, and is a floating city, home to more than 5,000 personnel. It is powered by two nuclear reactors that propel it through the water at more than 30 knots. But the one fact that impressed me most was how long the ship could remain at sea without any refueling whatsoever. Conventional aircraft carriers carried thousands of tons of fuel and needed regular refueling. The *Stennis,* on the other hand, needs to refuel only once every 26 years! In my mind, the most amazing property of a nuclear reactor is that you put just a little fuel in and you get an incredible amount of power out.

Solomon offers us our own personal power source to

drive us to our most distant and even impossible dreams, a power source that can transform a little bit of fuel into a tremendous amount of power. It requires the right kind of fuel, but our focus in this chapter is the power source itself. It can radically change any area of your life, and begin that change as soon as you begin to use it. It is so powerful that:

It enabled a first-grade dropout to receive more patents than anyone in history, including those for recording sound, movies, generating electricity, and, of course, the electric lightbulb.

It took a woman who lost her hearing and sight after her second birthday and transformed her from a bitter, hateful child into one of the most inspirational writers and speakers of the twentieth century.

It empowered a fifty-two-year-old salesman of milk-shake machines to quit his job and create the most successful restaurant franchise system in the world.

It enabled two college dropouts to turn a hole-in-the-wall start-up software company into one of the most highly valued companies in the world.

It literally turned a bookkeeper making ten cents an hour into the richest and most powerful man in the world.

I could fill this chapter and dozens more with stories of people who achieved their impossible dreams because of this power identified by King Solomon. That's how potent it is when it's applied to any important area of one's life. But this power source not only generates momentum, it provides direction as well. What is it? Solomon's power source is *vision*, and his fuel is *hope*. But don't be deceived by their simplicity. You'll discover that their combined power is like the power produced by splitting an atom.

◎◎ The Incredible Power of Vision and Hope

Solomon's concept of vision and hope is radically different from our contemporary concepts of these words. We hear the word "vision," and we picture something abstract such as a mystical experience or a dream. We hear the word "hope," and we instantly think of a wish or a desire. Our contemporary concepts of these two words fall woefully short of Solomon's concepts.

Vision is *not* something abstract or intangible, nor is hope a mere wish or desire. To Solomon, vision and hope are both tangible and precise. Understanding what Solomon meant when he used these two words is critical to achieving anything extraordinary with your life.

For most people, the word "vision" has little more relevance to their daily life than a modern-art painting has to choosing the highways they will follow when going on a vacation. By Solomon's definition, most people either have no vision at all for what they want in life, or the vision they have is vague and abstract (to be more successful, wealthier, etc.). To Solomon, a vision was not abstract at all. For him, gaining a true vision was more like using a highway atlas. It means having a perfectly clear picture of an ultimate destination, and a detailed road map to get there.

In my failed jobs after college, I never had a clear and precise vision of what I wanted to achieve. It's not surprising that they lasted less than a year or produced only minimal income. On the other hand, in my tenth job, I had a very clear vision for my first project. I created a detailed road map of my goals, and outlined the steps and tasks that I needed to complete to achieve those goals and fulfill that vision. The result? Within six months of starting the job, our sales skyrocketed from a thousand dollars a week to more than a million dollars a week.

But my life isn't the only example of a life that was radically changed by gaining a clear and precise vision. Thomas Edison was a first-grade dropout. His mother home-schooled him. Among other things, she taught him the Book of Proverbs. From his youth, he knew the importance of gaining a clear vision for whatever he wanted to accomplish and a detailed plan for accomplishing that vision. He used this "Vision Mapping Process" in pursuing every invention he tried to create. This process was such a tremendous source of creativity, persistence, and power that it enabled him to become the most prolific and successful innovator in history.

Gaining a clear and precise vision was what catapulted John D. Rockefeller from a ten-cents-an-hour bookkeeper to the richest man in the world. It transformed Helen Keller from a bitter young girl into one of the most inspirational speakers and writers of all time. It became the driving force that empowered Ray Kroc to look at a single tiny restaurant in San Bernardino, California, and transform it into the 25,000-franchise restaurant system of today's McDonald's.

That is the power of having a precise vision. Throughout their lives, each of these people talked about gaining a clear vision of what they wanted to achieve *before* they began the pursuit of their achievements.

A VISION is a precise, clearly defined goal with a detailed plan and timetable for achieving that goal.

◉◉ A Matter of Life and Death

How important is it that you have such well-defined "visions" in your personal and professional life? Solomon claims that it's *so* important that without it our innermost being will begin to waste away. The joy of living becomes replaced with the mere act of surviving, or "just getting by." You go from joy, to subsistence, to depression, and ultimately to despair. This is not the kind of life anyone should aspire to. We all want a life filled with happiness and extraordinary fulfillment, at home and at work. But, as Solomon says, "Where there is no vision, the people perish."

This Proverb applies to each area of our life. People often begin a job or career with a general idea or vision of what they hope to achieve. Whenever someone tells me how unhappy they are at work or in their marriage, all I have to do is ask them to tell me what their vision is for their job or marriage, and their root problem is instantly exposed. Inevitably, they have no vision. The good news is that gaining a clear and precise vision can bring renewed life to our dreams and innermost being.

๑๑ The Difference a Vision Makes

In 1879, a café-saloon owner in Dayton, Ohio, named James Ritty received a patent on a mechanical cash register that he designed to keep his employees from stealing money out of the till. Ritty created a company to hold the patent and sell his cash registers to other merchants. Unfortunately, he was able to sell only a few hundred units. When another merchant in Dayton, John Patterson, offered him $6,500 for his company and its patented invention, he was happy to sell. Ritty and the entire business community of Dayton thought Patterson was a sucker who had fallen off the turnip truck. They couldn't imagine paying so much money for an invention that had sold so little in the five years it had been on the market. But John Patterson had something that James Ritty and the other businessmen in Dayton didn't have: a vision. Before Patterson died, he sold more than 22 million cash registers, and his company became one of the most influential sales and marketing companies of all time. He named his company National Cash Register (NCR). According to one author, by 1984, one out of every six CEOs had received their initial training from NCR, including Thomas Watson, the founder of IBM.

๑๑ How Can YOU Gain a Vision for Your Top Priorities?

What do you want to achieve in your career or business? In your short-term and long-term finances? In your relationships with your spouse or children? If you haven't written down your dreams in each of these areas, I can promise you that there's almost no chance you'll ever achieve them. Earlier in this chapter, I mentioned the Vision Mapping Process. In the "Knowledge to Wisdom" section of this chapter, I will explain and illustrate it in more detail. Using this simple process, you will be able to gain a clear and precise vision for all of your most important dreams. You'll have a way to convert each vision into a set of specific goals, steps, and tasks. The result will be a clearly defined vision with a detailed road map and schedule that you can follow to achieve that vision.

As exciting as the Vision Mapping Process is, the real fulfillment that results from the Vision Mapping Process begins as you complete the tasks toward achieving your vision. Doing so will create an unexpected source of direction and the initial power to get "un-stuck," as well as help you gain the momentum you need to complete your journey. The power to achieve your dreams is supplied by Solomon's fuel—hope. But Solomon's definition of hope is quite different from how we normally think of it. In the next chapter, we'll uncover the true meaning of hope and discover how to ignite this high-octane fuel and harness its power.

The Vision Mapping Process will not only work for you; it will work for those around you as well: your employees, your spouse, and your children. As you help them define their dreams and achieve their goals, their level of fulfillment and motivation will skyrocket.

When Carol, my oldest daughter, was eleven, Michael Landon asked her what she was going to be when she grew up. "The first woman on the Philadelphia Phillies baseball team," she replied. Mike laughed and gave me a nudge. I told Carol to tell him how she was going to do that. "Daddy says when we have a dream, we need to convert it into specific goals. So my goals are to become the best fielder and hitter on my softball team. He says you then have to convert your goals into steps; so my steps are to practice fielding each day and hitting once a week. He says that we then have to convert our steps into tasks; so Dad has to come home every night by six to play catch with me and take me to the batting cage on Saturdays." Although Carol never did join the Phillies, her improvement was so significant that her coach asked her what she was doing. When she told him, he told the other girls on the team, and they began doing the same. The result? Their team went from being the worst team in the league (all losses) in their first season to winning the league championship with all "wins" the next season. Same girls, same coach. That's the power of the Vision Mapping Process . . . even with eleven-year-olds.

Knowledge to Wisdom

USING THE VISION MAPPING PROCESS TO ESTABLISH A ROAD MAP TO ACHIEVE YOUR DREAMS

The Vision Mapping Process is a goal-achieving process that will radically increase your productivity and raise the level of your achievement in any endeavor, project, or area of life to which it is applied. First, it helps you to create a clear and specific vision, along with a detailed road map to effectively and quickly achieve that vision. It infuses life into any area in which it is applied.

There are five steps in the Vision Mapping Process. As you turn to these steps, you'll need to have a loose-leaf notebook and pen at hand. Or you can get a "Vision Mapping Journal" at my Web site (www.stevenkscott.com), with all of the necessary tabbed sections and preprinted forms needed to Vision Map your dreams in every important area of your life.

With your journal in hand, write down a list of the areas of your life in which you would like to see significant improvement. Some people will list only a couple of areas (such as "personal life" and "career"). Others will have more. There is no magic number. For example, my areas are: my marriage, my children, my health, my business, and extracurricular projects. Once you've determined your most important areas, write them down. Next, make a list of your most important dreams, desires, or projects for those areas in your life. Next, prioritize each list, starting with your most important dream.

Once you've done this, you're ready to begin the Vision Mapping Process.

1. Starting with your most important dream in any given area, write a clear and precise description of that dream. This description should be at least a sentence or two, but no more than a single page. If possible, try to draw or find a picture that provides you with an image or symbol of what fulfilling this dream might look like.

2. Create a "Goals Page" for that specific dream. To do this, state the dream at the top of the page. Then make a list of the specific, intermediate "goals" that need to be achieved to fulfill that dream. This step converts your dreams into specific goals.

3. Create a page for each goal and label those pages "Goals to Steps." On each page, list the intermediate goal you want to achieve, then list the steps that need to be taken to achieve that goal.

4. Next, take any complex step in your list of steps that requires the completion of more than one task, and create a "Steps to Tasks" page. List the specific tasks that need to be completed to take that step.

5. The final step in this process is to assign completion dates to each task and step. Once you've done that, you are ready to begin. Now you can work on achieving each goal one task or step at a time. Complete each step, one by one, until you have achieved your dream.

This process will likely reveal tasks or steps that you cannot complete on your own, due to lack of know-how or limited resources. Don't panic. As you'll see in Chapter 6, partnering is the single most powerful strategy that you will employ in the pursuit of your dreams, and you can become an expert at it!

Do I Really Have to Write All of This Out?

That's the first question everyone asks when I share this process with an audience. The answer is yes. Remember that you want to create a clear and precise vision for each of your dreams, and a detailed road map and timetable for achieving those dreams. That's what this process will give you. If it looks like an overwhelming project, it's not. One to five minutes a day is all it takes for the writing part of this process. You don't do everything at once. There's no deadline on completing your Vision Mapping. It's a lifetime project. You could literally apply this process to one dream a week, a month, or a year. This single process will enable you to experience all of the power of Solomon's strategy for gaining a vision and converting that vision into reality. Doing so will give you the power to achieve those dreams.

CHAPTER 4

Solomon's Power Secret for Turning Dreams into Reality

Hope deferred makes the heart sick:
but desire fulfilled is a tree of life.

—PROVERBS 13:12

๑๑ Mankind's Perpetual Fuel

For more than a hundred years, engineers and scientists have dreamed of a perpetual source of energy, one that would generate more power than it consumes. Imagine a power source that would drive your car without ever needing to be replenished. The truth is, a perpetual source of energy would violate the known laws of physics. But there is a source of perpetual mental and emotional fuel available to us to achieve our dreams. It is called "hope."

Today we usually use it as a synonym for a wish. Yet to Solomon, hope was far more tangible and powerful. His concept of hope can be defined as "a well-founded and confident belief that a specific vision (goal, desire, or promise) will be achieved or fulfilled within a specified amount of time."

HOPE is a *well-founded* and *confident belief* that a specific vision (goal, desire, or promise) will be achieved or fulfilled within a specified amount of time.

Think about it. How can you have a "well-founded, confident belief that a specific vision will be achieved" if you don't have a specific vision? If your visions or desires are general or vague instead of well-defined, you cannot gain or sustain any genuine hope of achieving them. This is why the Vision Mapping Process is so important. It becomes the basis or foundation for gaining what I call true hope. Knowing where you want to go, and having a precise map on hand to get there, fuels your efforts in achieving your vision.

As you complete each step toward achieving a goal, more hope is produced to help you achieve the next step. In other words, true hope becomes the fuel that keeps you moving toward the ultimate fulfillment of a vision. And each step you complete drives you even more powerfully and quickly toward the achievement of your vision. In a sense, hope is mankind's only perpetual fuel. Hope produces progress toward a given goal, and your progress produces even more hope and greater momentum.

The Vision Mapping Process helps to give us that initial hope, because by using it, we can see our destination clearly and realize how to get there.

☺ Procrastination Can Be Toxic

On the other hand, if we fail to take those steps and complete those tasks toward our goal, hope can be put off or, as Solomon said, "deferred." When hope is deferred, it begins to slip away. And guess what happens? As Solomon wrote in Proverbs 13:12, "Hope deferred makes the heart sick: but desire fulfilled is a tree of life." When hope is put off, you lose your emotional energy and your motivation. Your creativity and productivity begin to plummet. You withdraw. Sooner or later, you give up on the vision or dream altogether. Give up too many dreams, and living becomes little more than just getting by.

We create the seeds of hope in others by stating or implying commitments. These commitments create a vision. If we fail to fulfill those commitments in a timely manner, we then defer others' hope. They lose their energy and motivation. Moreover, they lose their trust in us. The consequences of deferring hope in others can even lead to the death of a relationship.

☺ Deferring Hope on the Job

When managers defer the hope of their employees, their creativity, productivity, motivation, and commitment gradually decline, and ultimately begin to plummet. Henry Ford had a vision for making automobiles that any family could afford. When he was recruited to be the chief engineer of the fledgling Detroit Automobile Company, he was told by the board to put his vision on hold. They wanted to design and manufacture cars for the only known buyers of the day, the wealthy. Ford's true hopes were deferred, and in two years he and his company failed to put a single car into the marketplace. He was fired. The next year he founded Ford, and instead of deferring his hopes, the board supported his vision and allowed him to fulfill his desire. His "fulfilled desire" truly became a "tree of life"— to him, his company, his employees, his customers, our nation, and the world. By 1928, one out of every two cars in the world was a Ford.

On my first job, my boss told me that if I made lots of sales calls and used the sales techniques he had taught me, I would make lots of sales. He told me my commission checks would soon be much greater than my small salary. I worked very hard to master the sales techniques he taught. I made lots of sales calls. Unfortunately, I did not make lots of sales. My salary was $500 a month; after six months of selling, my commissions were less than $40 a month. My expectations had been raised too high, my hopes shattered. I left that job after only seven months.

On my third job, my boss told me that if I performed the routine analytical part of my job well, he would start to involve me in the creative and advertising side of our department. I've always become quickly bored with anything routine and have always loved creative work. By the end of my first month, I had my analytical responsibilities mastered and running smoothly. When I asked my boss if I could start working with the creative people, he gave me a condescending look and turned me down. The hope he had initially instilled within me had been quickly deferred. My heart grew sick. I showed up for work every day and gave him exactly what he wanted—routine analysis. I gave him no more . . . and no less. Instead of bringing my creativity to the job, I began searching for other creative outlets, moonlighting for other corporate executives in different subsidiaries of our company. Without my boss's knowledge, I applied for a job with one of the company's other subsidiaries and was granted a transfer.

Upon hearing of my impending transfer, my boss fired me and humiliated me in front of our entire department. As far as he was concerned, my creative talents were worthless. Three years after leaving his company, I produced a television marketing campaign for his company as an outside vendor. It became the single most profitable marketing campaign in his company's history. But instead of paying me the $12,000 annual salary he paid when I worked for him, his company paid my partners and me millions of dollars. Had he not "deferred my hope," he could have had the same creative ideas from me for a tiny fraction of the cost. Worse, he received almost no credit for this campaign from the board of directors of his company. Instead, the credit went to the "outside vendor" (our company). The lesson? If you want loyalty, creativity, and productivity from those who work with you, don't defer the hopes and dreams you are responsible for creating. You must learn how to incorporate this Proverb into your job.

෨ Poisoning Your Marriage, One Day at a Time
I recently saw a documentary about a woman who was caught

trying to poison her third husband. She had successfully poisoned the first two husbands a few years earlier by putting a tiny amount of arsenic in each meal. Over a six-month period each husband became more and more sick. And both of them died. The woman's third husband became suspicious about his growing illness and he caught his wife on videotape, sprinkling a little powder onto his meal. She was caught and later prosecuted for the murders of her previous husbands.

When you defer the hope of your spouse in any important area, it's like adding a little poison to each meal. It doesn't bring instant death, but it gradually makes their heart sick. They begin to lose their motivation, their energy level drops, and they ultimately become demoralized. They lose their joy, their trust in you, their commitment to you, and their motivation to be with you. They begin to withdraw from you, and quiet resentment builds in their heart. Your marriage begins to die. It may survive legally, but its life will disappear.

◉◉ Deferring Hope in Marriage

Men often defer the hopes of their wives in several critical areas, and women often unconsciously return the favor. According to relationship expert Dr. Gary Smalley, the four greatest needs of a woman are: (1) emotional and physical security, (2) the need for regular meaningful communication, (3) nonsexual touch, and (4) romance. Each night when a husband comes home, his wife (sometimes without even knowing it) hopes that these needs will be addressed and fulfilled. They want to feel the security of his love and commitment; the safety of being able to express their feelings and opinions without being interrupted or criticized. They want to be held and caressed without it being linked to the husband's need for sex. They want to be listened to and have the chance to talk about their day. They want to be able to talk about their hopes, desires, and dreams. They want to hear about their husband's day. They want to feel connected. And, they want to be romanced. They want to feel valued for who they are, not just what they do.

And how do husbands defer their hopes? Too often, the last thing most men want when they come home is to engage in "meaningful conversation." So they put it off, deferring that hope. They tend to defer their wives' hopes of romance until Valentine's Day or until they want something. What's so tragic is that men don't just defer their hopes once in a while, but regularly. In addition to deferring their wives' hopes in the areas of their greatest needs, men defer their hopes in lesser areas. Every woman wants her husband's help around the house. She wants him to help with the kids. Here again, many men defer their hopes more often than they fulfill them.

๑ How Women Can Return the Favor

But men often have their hopes deferred as well. According to Dr. Smalley, the greatest needs of a man are (1) to feel respected and admired, (2) to be loved and desired, and (3) to enjoy sexual intimacy regularly and consistently. His hope is that his intimate encounters with his wife will reflect her desire rather than her obligation. Unfortunately, this hope is often deferred unless he first fulfills his wife's hopes and needs.

This difference in expectation can create all sorts of "deferred hopes" in a marriage, making happiness and fulfillment between a man and a woman more difficult . . . unless each one begins to make the other's hopes and needs a top priority, taking the initiative to fulfill their hopes rather than deferring them.

Solomon's Solution

While deferring hope makes the heart sick, there's GREAT news in the second half of this same Proverb. It reads "but desire fulfilled, is a tree of life."

When I was recruited for my tenth job, I would have been happy to work for the salary I was given. But my boss was wiser than that. In addition to my salary, he gave me a percentage of our new company. In contrast to my previous nine jobs, this was the first where I had been given a "piece of the action." The result? Prior to my arrival, his company was earning about $100,000 a year in profits on gross sales of less than a million dollars per year. The first marketing campaign I created (three months after I was hired) generated an additional $20 million in sales and $3 million in earnings.

He followed the same pattern with our other key employees, making them partners in the business. Together, we've generated billions in sales and $150 million in earnings. My boss and his children became multimillionaires. This would never have happened had he not offered us ownership. By fulfilling "my unspoken desires," he planted a tree of life that created tremendous benefit for all of us.

We can bring a whole new source of energy into our work, our marriages, and our lives when we stop deferring hopes and begin to focus on helping others fulfill their genuine needs and dreams and desires. Doing so will bring a new level of joy and fulfillment into their lives. It will increase their morale, their commitment, and their trust. And their creativity and productivity will explode.

◎◎ Fanning the Flames of Hope

If your heart has been made sick by deferred hope, you must do all you can to restore its health as soon as possible. Remember, hope is deferred in two ways. First, it is deferred when others do not fulfill their promises or commitments to you within the time frame that you thought they would. Second, it is deferred by your own lack of clear and precise visions for your important dreams.

Gaining a clear and precise vision of your dreams will bring a whole new level of fulfillment to your life. Apply the Vision Mapping Process to the pursuit of your dreams. You'll find that you will begin to achieve each dream in a timely manner. And with each desire, dream, or goal that is accomplished, your level of fulfillment will skyrocket. You will experience firsthand Solomon's promise in Proverbs 13:19: "Desire accomplished is sweet to the soul . . ."

Knowledge to Wisdom

1. Make a list of some of your greatest hopes that have been deferred as a result of the actions of others.

2. List any hopes that have not been realized due to your own lack of a clear and precise vision.

3. List some of the hopes of others that you have deferred. (Ask your spouse, your children, or those you work with. They'll be glad to help you.)

4. List the hopes that you would like to pursue by creating a vision map.

5. Ask your spouse what his or her greatest hopes are. Offer to help create a vision map to pursue those hopes.

6. Ask your children what their important hopes are. Help them to create a vision map to pursue those hopes.

CHAPTER 5

The Key That Opens Any Door

> The heart of the wise teaches his mouth,
> and adds persuasiveness to his lips.
>
> —PROVERBS 16:23

Last year, my wife, Shannon, bought a new car that had many features we had never seen before. One in particular has turned out to be quite convenient. It's an electronic key that doesn't need to be inserted into the door to unlock it, nor into the ignition to start the car. It doesn't even need to leave her purse. As she walks up to the door, the door automatically unlocks itself. When she sits down in the car, she still doesn't take the key out of her purse. She simply puts her foot on the car's brake pedal and pushes a button on the gearshift knob, and the car immediately starts. It does that because the key has a built-in receiver and transmitter. When her hand touches the door handle, or she sits in the driver's seat, the car sends out a signal that the key receives. The key then transmits an encoded signal back to the door lock or to the starter, depending on whether she's outside or in the seat. Is that a cool key, or what?

Well, as cool as Shannon's key is, it can't even begin to compare to Solomon's key. Solomon's key can open any door and activate any ignition in the world. It can open the door to the minds of your employer or your potential customers; it can open your banker's vault and the wallets of your investors. It can open the hearts and minds of your spouse and children. I'm talking about Solomon's key of effective communication.

ೞ Ineffective Communication—The Number-One Problem in Business and Life

Whether at work or at home, most ideas are ignored or rejected not because they're bad ideas but because they're ineffectively or unpersuasively communicated. According to a survey of business owners and corporate CEOs, ineffective communication is the number-one problem in business; according to Dr. Gary Smalley, it is also the number-one problem in relationships. As you master the communication skills that Solomon offers, you will be able to achieve levels of success on your job that far exceed the potential of those who lack these skills.

At home, the impact of becoming an effective communicator is even greater. In most families, communication can be destructive as often as it is beneficial. Men and women are guilty of saying the wrong things at the wrong time—or, equally bad, not saying anything at all. The fact that most women are right-brain dominant (the feeling side of the brain) and most men are left-brain dominant (the factual, analytical side of the brain) in itself creates a communication barrier that can be challenging.

According to communication experts, while most women speak an average of 25,000 to 50,000 words a day, most men speak only 12,000 to 25,000 words a day. This dynamic creates more "mis-connections." One of the greatest needs of a woman, according to Dr. Smalley, is the need to "feel connected." Without effective two-way communication, the connection a couple felt earlier in their relationship begins to dissipate. Before long, they don't feel connected at all.

What we say, and how we say it, can have a life-changing impact on others.

I wrote my first direct-response television commercial in 1976. A direct-response television commercial is one that sells a product directly to the consumer. It does this by providing a toll-free telephone number, address, or Web address that enables the consumer to place an order for the product immediately following the commercial, without having to purchase that product from a retail store. Selling a product through this means is not as easy as it sounds. You only have 60 to 120 seconds to grab the viewer's attention, create curiosity about the product, demonstrate the product, differentiate the product from any other product on the market, overcome the viewer's skepticism and excuses for not buying the product, motivate them to immediately place an order, and enable them to memorize the phone number or write it down. Fewer than one out of every 100 direct-response commercials succeed. Yet, in the first ten years of our business, of the commercials I wrote, our success rate was over 70 percent. They generated more than 25 million phone calls to order our company's goods and services. That demonstrates the incredible power of effective and persuasive communication.

As impressive as this might be, it can't even begin to compare to the power that Solomon talks about in communicating with others. For Solomon is talking about every aspect of our communication: our words, our tone of voice, our gestures and facial expressions, our spirit, our timing, and all the nonverbal communication cues that frame our comments.

Your communication can extinguish anger or escalate it.

A soft answer turns away wrath but grievous words stir up anger. —Proverbs 15:1

Whenever we are angry, or we encounter someone who is, we have a choice to make: Do we want to turn up the heat and help fuel the fire, or do we want to turn down the heat and extinguish the flames? Our natural inclination is always to follow the path of least resistance. If I am the angry person, my natural inclination is to let my anger spin out of control. If someone else is angry, our natural inclination is to return like for like. If they're using cutting remarks, we'll attempt to cut them down. If they raise their voice or yell, we raise our voice louder. Unfortunately, according to Solomon, responding to anger with anger only intensifies and escalates the damage. But we don't have to follow our natural inclinations. We can throw cold water on our anger, or anyone else's, by simply injecting kind words, a soft tone of voice, and gentleness in our tone and approach.

My wife and children would tell you that I can lose my temper as easily as the next person. However, as soon as I realize what's happening, I begin to hear Solomon's Proverb echoing in my ear: "A soft answer turns away wrath, but grievous words stir up anger." I then have to make a choice: Do I continue to use harsh words and escalate the anger, or do I choose calming words, a soft tone of voice, and more gentle gestures? Nearly every time I have turned to softness, anger has been dispelled. When I'm the one who is angry, I'm almost instantly calmed. When someone else is angry at me, it may take a minute or so of such effort to calm them down, but rarely more than that. A while back, one of my partners became angry with me during a conference call. Rather than yelling back at him, I simply lowered my voice and forced myself to calmly and quietly answer his argument. He instantly lowered his volume, changed his tone of voice, and listened to me rather than attack me.

With four children at home, a day rarely passes without at least one argument. I never cease to be amazed at how quickly they calm down when I speak softly. Often, there's an instant de-escalation. When you first begin using this tactic, don't be discouraged if your calming reply doesn't elicit an immediate result. Sometimes a person may be so enraged that you may need to respond gently to them for several minutes before they begin to calm down.

A word of caution: If you have done something that the

other person considers extremely offensive, they may see your initial efforts to speak in softer language and a softer tone of voice as a form of condescension, or denial of responsibility. This is where your choice of words must show that you understand the degree of your offense and demonstrate a sincere desire to make things right.

Your communication can wound others or heal them.

There is [he] that speaketh like the piercings of a sword: but the tongue of the wise is health. —*Proverbs 12:18*

Nearly every parent I know desires to build the self-esteem and emotional health of their children. And yet I have seen countless parents throw verbal daggers at their children. Sometimes the cuts are inflicted subtly, by tone of voice and implication; at other times, they are hurled with real force. Regardless, such wounds, although "only words," can scar your child for life. Parents often think their kids are unaffected by harsh words, or that "children are resilient." Sometimes parents excuse their own harsh words by claiming they were "just telling the truth," and if the truth hurts, so be it! As we'll see a little later, there are a thousand wrong ways to criticize and, according to Solomon, only one right way. The wrong ways inflict deep wounds; the right way usually leaves no wound at all.

During a recent PBS television appearance, I asked the audience, "How many of you can remember a specific criticism you received from your parents when you were a child that deeply hurt you?" Nearly every hand in the audience shot up. Even elderly audience members could recall criticisms from their youth, sixty or seventy years before. That's how powerful hurtful words can be. Their imprint on one's mind may never be erased.

Solomon says that a wise man or woman will use communication to bring healing and health to others. In Proverbs 16:24, he writes, "Pleasant words are as an honeycomb, sweet to the soul, and health to the bones." Earlier, in Proverbs 12:25, he says, "Heaviness in the heart of man makes it stoop: but a good word makes it glad." Words of praise, appreciation, encouragement, and understanding can penetrate one's mind and heal one's very soul.

If you're skeptical about the impact encouraging words can have on one's physical health, *USA Today* reported that two medical studies showed that depression and stress increase inflammation in the circulatory system, a major risk factor in heart disease and heart attacks. One of these studies suggested the reverse: The stronger a person's relationships are, and the happier they are, the lower their levels of inflammation. Remember that Solomon said that pleasant words are "health to the bones." Bone marrow, of course, is the source of our red blood cells and much of our immune system. Without the advantage of microbiology or clinical studies, Solomon was right on target.

Your communication can infuse life into a person's spirit.
A wholesome tongue is a tree of life.   —*Proverbs 15:4*

The Hebrew word for wholesome literally translates to "healing" or "curative." In other words, Solomon is saying that a healing tongue is a "tree of life." I love this expression, because trees, of course, are not only alive, they provide life to others. Their leaves provide us with oxygen to breathe, their fruit provides us with food to eat, and their roots provide stability to our soil. The same is true of a person who communicates with healing words. His encouraging communication improves not only his life but the lives of those around him.

The opposite, however, is also true. Communication that is "perverse," in Solomon's words, can fracture one's spirit. The word he uses—"perverseness therein is a breach of spirit"—literally means distortion or viciousness. When we communicate in a way that is dishonest or verbally vicious, we run the risk of breaking a person's spirit. When a person's spirit is broken by another, not only does the relationship suffer, but the person can be emotionally scarred forever.

Many years ago, a close friend of mine divorced her husband, apparently after years of physical and verbal abuse. What particularly struck me was that she claimed the verbal abuse was much more painful than the physical abuse. Years after her divorce, she told me, "The physical bruises and cuts healed in a matter of days, but the emotional pain and scars are with me even today."

Throughout our lives, we are faced with opportunities to communicate in ways that either foster healing and health or inflict pain. *Most people have no idea just how much power resides in what they say and how they say it.* Choose your words, and how you frame them, wisely.

Your communication can save a life or take a life.

**Death and life are in the power of the tongue: and they that
love it shall eat the fruit thereof.   —Proverbs 18:21**

Perhaps one of the most vivid examples of the "tongue's
power" to save life took place in Atlanta, Georgia, in March
2005. Brian Nichols had murdered a judge and three others
when he took Ashley Smith hostage and forced her to let him
into her apartment. Most of America knows the rest of the
story. Her words of hope, vision, and purpose, and the words
she read from the book *The Purpose-Driven Life,* brought about
a dynamic change in the heart and mind of her captor. Her
words not only saved her life, they saved his life and who
knows how many other lives that might have been lost had he
not peacefully surrendered to the police.

My best friend, Jim Shaughnessy, has spent a lifetime
using his words to bring life to others. The moment he walks
into the room, people seem to cheer up. Whether they are a
child or an adult, Jim seems to know just what to say to make
them feel happy and appreciated. As a result, he has more
close friendships than anyone I have ever known.

Your communication can bring delight to others.

A word fitly spoken is like apples of gold in pictures of silver.

—Proverbs 25:11

Have you ever seen a beautiful painting or photograph
that stopped you dead in your tracks? Imagine the incredible
works of art that must have filled Solomon's palace. Judging

from this Proverb, I'll bet he had a particular piece of art that was his favorite, one that brought delight to him and to his guests—a picture or sculpture crafted in silver, decorated with apples of gold. Yet as beautiful and desirable as that picture might have been, Solomon says that speaking the right words at the right time is just as beautiful and worthwhile. Moreover, when such words are expressed, the speaker or writer is deeply appreciated by the other person. I have been fortunate throughout my life to be surrounded by people who seem to know just what to say and how and when to say it. In my times of sadness or despair, my wife, Shannon, and my best friends, Jim and Patty Shaughnessy, Tom and Marlene Delnoce, the Smalleys, and my partners, Bob, John, and Dave Marsh, have always found words that have become apples of gold in pictures of silver, words that could draw my attention away from my pain and lift my soul and spirit. In such times, my appreciation and love for them increased all the more.

We all have the ability to provide such words of love, kindness, encouragement, and wisdom. Solomon gives us a number of ways to increase the power of our words and communications.

◎◎ Solomon's Keys to Communication

Solomon's keys to maximizing the power of our communication seem like common sense at first glance, but in fact they are anything *but* common today.

1. Speak in Such a Way That You Make Others Want to Listen

The tongue of the wise makes knowledge acceptable, But the mouth of fools spouts folly. —*Proverbs 15:2*

For most people, speaking means simply saying whatever they feel like saying. People say what they think or feel as they think or feel it, regardless of its validity or appropriateness. When you have something that you really want the other person to clearly understand and embrace, you need to communicate it in a *way* that makes it palatable. A wise man or woman does whatever it takes to make what they have to say easy to swallow.

2. Learn to Become Persuasive

The heart of the wise teaches his mouth and adds persuasiveness to his lips. —*Proverbs 16:23*

The Hebrew word Solomon uses for "teaches" in Proverbs 16:23 literally means "to instruct" or "thoughtfully guide." In other words, don't talk every time you feel like talking; instead, take control of what you say. Learn when to speak and when not to speak. You should think about when to speak and what to say before you open your mouth. For some, this is easy. For others, it can be very difficult. One obvious benefit is that when you are not talking, you can listen, and listening gives you a better understanding of the other person's perspective and point of view.

The second half of Solomon's injunction in this Proverb tells us to add persuasiveness to our speech. People sometimes equate persuasiveness with manipulation. Nothing could be further from the truth. Manipulation uses any means possible, including deceit, to convince someone to do something that is not in their best interest. Persuasion, on the other hand, allows you to present your point of view in a clear and compelling way to motivate someone to do what you believe to be in their best interest or for the common good.

3. Listen Before Speaking

> *He that answers a matter before he hears it, it is folly and*
> *shame unto him.*   —*Proverbs 18:13*

Whenever we begin to answer a person before the person finishes making his point, we are both foolish and rude. One of my dearest friends has always had a habit of speaking before I completely finish a thought. It's as if he's trying to finish my statement for me. Sadly, he usually jumps to the wrong conclusion. He is such a kind man that I can't consider him rude, but his doing so is certainly an error of judgment. I've been guilty of doing the same thing with my partners, my friends, my wife, and my children. Even though I don't mean to be rude, that is how I can come across. Why risk this when we can just patiently wait for the person to finish speaking?

4. Be Slow to Speak, and Guard Your Words Carefully

> *Do you see a man who is hasty in his words? There is more*
> *hope for a fool than for him.*   —*Proverbs 29:20*

Why was the wisest and richest man who ever lived so repetitive and insistent that we guard our mouth and be "slow to speak"? I believe it's because as king he sat in the company of many who pretended to be wise, but whose words exposed them as fools. I'm sure he witnessed many who were quick to speak, and spoke foolishly. Once words leave our lips, they can never be retracted. Solomon, more than anyone, knew the incredible power that words can carry. In Proverbs 13:3, he wrote, "The one who guards his mouth preserves his life; The one who opens wide his lips comes to ruin." I have known men whose unwise words have gotten them fired and destroyed their careers.

5. Never Tear Others Down—Rather, Build Them Up

It is so easy to say things that are cutting or hurtful to others, whether we say it to their face or behind their back. We rationalize this with the excuse that everyone else does it, too. But there is nothing innocent about cutting somebody with a sword. Yet that's exactly what Solomon says we are doing when we cut somebody down with words (Proverbs 12:18). A wise man or woman, he says, uses words to build others up, to heal their wounds and fortify their self-esteem. Our natural inclination is to join in on the office gossip, or use angry words to defend ourselves when under attack. Solomon urges us to *choose* to act contrary to our natural inclinations, refusing to take part in gossip and avoiding the use of words that would hurt others. He urges us to replace negative words with positive ones. When someone gossips about another, instead of joining in, say a few positive things about that person. You'll be amazed at how quickly the conversation turns from the negative to the positive.

6. Stop While You're Ahead

When there are many words, transgression is unavoidable,
But he who restrains his lips is wise. —*Proverbs 10:19*

Many people, once they start talking, have a hard time stopping. I'm one of them. Solomon warns that when you keep talking after you've made your point, you're likely to say something foolish. This has happened to me on countless occasions. Make your point briefly, and then be silent. As Proverbs 17:28 states, even a fool is considered wise when he keeps silent. And he who makes a strong point with only a few words is highly esteemed by those around him.

7. Share Genuine Wisdom

The mouth of the just brings forth wisdom.

—*Proverbs 10:31a*

With Solomon's emphasis on saying less, here is one area where he encourages us to say more. True wisdom is a rare commodity in today's culture. When someone genuinely has something worthwhile to say, Solomon encourages them to share it. Grandfathers and grandmothers, fathers and mothers, mentors and managers should be generous in sharing the wisdom of their experience with their children and grandchildren, their employees, and those they work with.

8. Always Speak Truthfully

He that hideth hatred with lying lips, and he that uttereth a
slander, is a fool. —*Proverbs 10:18*

A recent survey of human resources managers revealed that a high percentage of job applicants exaggerate or outright lie on their résumés. The same is true in marketing—there is little truth in advertising, it often seems. Ads in all media exaggerate benefits and minimize risks to prospective consumers. Outright lying seems to be pervasive even at the top of some of America's largest and most admired corporations.

When people lie, they think they're outwitting the other person. The fact is, however, according to Solomon, it's *never* smart to lie. Executives at Enron, Tyco, and WorldCom thought they were being smart with their "creative accounting." But they were really just lying with numbers. Their lies cost them and their employees and shareholders dearly. Even "little lies" can have big consequences, as Martha Stewart can attest.

If lying is foolishness, telling the truth is smart. It creates a foundation of integrity that we can build our life and reputation upon. It shows our spouses, children, friends, employers, peers, and customers that they can rely on us.

◎◎ The Benefits of Becoming an Effective Communicator

Solomon promises three additional rewards for those who become effective and persuasive communicators.

1. Material Success

> ***The lips of the righteous feed many.***   —*Proverbs 10:21*

Steven Spielberg and I sat next to each other at many of our high school football games. While neither one of us had stood out in high school, both of us achieved our "impossible dreams" as adults. Eighteen years after we graduated, when we finally met up again, I discovered that our lives had been turned around by the same factors. We had both gained a clear and precise vision of what we wanted to achieve, we had both found terrific mentors and partners, and we both had learned how to effectively and persuasively communicate.

If you're thinking, "Yeah, but you're the exception," you're wrong. Just as ineffective communication is one of the greatest problems in life, when you *effectively* communicate, it produces tremendous benefits for you and those you associate with. In Proverbs 18:20, Solomon says, "A man's belly shall be satisfied with the fruit of his mouth; and with the increase of his lips shall he be filled."

2. Joy and Fulfillment

A man hath joy by the answer of his mouth: and a word spoken in due season, how good is it!   —*Proverbs 15:23*

Whenever I express something to someone else that I know will be beneficial, I feel a sense of satisfaction. When I say something that relieves one of my children's hurts or concerns, I feel a deep sense of joy. Solomon says that when we say the right words at the right time we get that Jackie Gleason feeling of "How sweet it is." In Proverbs 12:14, Solomon says that "a man will be satisfied with good by the fruit of his words." Isn't it gratifying to know that offering wise words can not only make a positive difference in the lives of others but can also bring greater satisfaction, joy, and fulfillment into our lives as well?

3. The Friendship of Those Around You

He that loves pureness of heart, for the grace of his lips the
king shall be his friend.   —Proverbs 22:11

Who *wouldn't* like to have the respect, appreciation, and friendship of others? Solomon promises this and more to those who love virtue, and whose virtue is expressed in conversation that is kind and gracious. Even "kings" will be his friends. I have never met a king, but I have enjoyed friendships with some of America's finest entertainers, and leaders in business and government. And today, such networking can make an invaluable contribution to anyone's career. Like everyone else, people in authority would much rather associate with someone they can trust. Your integrity and ability to effectively communicate creates a foundation upon which friendship at all levels can be built.

◎◎ How to Make Knowledge Acceptable and Add Persuasiveness to Your Lips

Solomon directs us to become persuasive communicators and to use communication in a way that "makes knowledge acceptable." The question is, "how?" How can we communicate effectively and persuasively? For 30 years, I have used three techniques that have proved to be incredibly powerful. They've enabled me to generate millions of toll-free phone calls in response to my two-minute commercials and generate billions of dollars in sales. Because I do not have the space in this chapter to teach these techniques. I would refer you to the two chapters I have written on communication in my book *Mentored by a Millionaire*. Or you can find a summary of these techniques and other communication skills on my Web site: www.stevenkscott.com.

Knowledge to Wisdom

How we communicate is so much a part of who we are, yet we often pay less attention than we should to how and what we communicate. At the end of your day, think back over what you said at various points to get a clear picture of what you're doing right and what you're doing wrong in communicating with others, whether at work or at home. Do this for one week. Then write out how you can change the negative ways you communicate, and increase the positive.

MY DAILY COMMUNICATION CHECKLIST

DID I:

___ Use "soft" answers to de-escalate tension, anger, or arguments?

___ Use cutting words to tear someone down?

___ Use encouraging words to build someone up?

___ Say the right thing at just the right time to help encourage or support someone?

___ Find ways to make knowledge acceptable?

___ Use persuasiveness rather than authority or force to make my argument?

___ Listen well before I spoke, or did I answer before I listened?

___ Communicate wisdom and fairness?

WAS I:

___ Slow to speak, or hasty to express my thoughts?

___ Truthful, without exaggeration, or misleading?

CHAPTER 6

The Great Accelerator: The Key to Maximum Success in Minimum Time

Without counsel plans are frustrated,
but with many counselors they succeed.

—PROVERBS 15:22

ෙ◎ Why Pursue Your Dreams at 5 mph When You Can Go 65?

Shortly after I received my driver's license, I was driving my sister's car on a freeway in Phoenix. A car in front of me was moving too slowly for my comfort, so I switched lanes to pass and hit the gas pedal as hard as I could to get around the other car. As a new driver, I loved the exhilaration of putting the pedal to the metal and feeling the car instantly respond with quick acceleration. Only this time, something was dreadfully wrong. As I tromped on the pedal, nothing happened. I didn't even hear the engine rev up. I kept stomping on the pedal as hard as I could, but nothing happened! Worse, the car was slowing down. I glanced at the fuel gauge and to my horror saw that the needle was pointed to the E. If you have ever run out of gas, you know the feeling. But the feeling that stuck with me most clearly was the feeling of helplessness I experienced when I pressed repeatedly on the accelerator to no response.

Now imagine if a car didn't have an accelerator. Even the world's fastest and most expensive sports car would be worthless. No matter how powerful its fuel and engine, without an accelerator, the engine would only idle. On the other hand, with an accelerator, a car not only moves forward, it can accelerate to high speeds, allowing you to arrive at your destination quickly. Without Solomon's accelerator, you will never achieve any extraordinary dream in a reasonable amount of time. In fact, you're likely to give up on your dreams altogether, just idling alone without making significant progress. Most people just give up. Solomon's accelerator changes everything. When correctly used, it will move you toward the achievement of your goals and dreams at unimaginable speeds.

Unfortunately, most people go through life without effectively applying this accelerator in the pursuit of their dreams. They simply idle. The fact is, every superachiever in history has used this accelerator to achieve their dreams. And *no one* in history has achieved any significant or extraordinary achievement without using this accelerator. What is this accelerator? It is Solomon's strategy of effective partnering.

๑๑ What's a Partner?

In Chapter 2, we saw that one of Solomon's four steps to bringing diligence into any area of your life is that of effectively partnering. You literally can't be truly diligent in any important endeavor without partnering. In Solomon's writings, he uses a number of words to convey the concept of partnering, but more often than not, he uses the words "counselor" and "counsel." I like his choice of words, because they have a much broader connotation than our modern concept of a partner. When we think of a partner, we usually think of a legal partner. A counselor, on the other hand, can mean anyone who gives us needed advice, consultation, direction, or aid in the pursuit of a particular goal. It can be a legal partner, but it can also be a friend, a spouse, a coworker, a key employee, an adviser, a mentor, or even an author. By this definition, when you study the Book of Proverbs, you are making Solomon your counselor. And when you follow his advice, you are truly acting as if he's your partner. In other words, you have the privilege of having in your camp the richest and wisest man who ever lived.

A PARTNER OR COUNSELOR is anyone who can provide needed insight, advice, wisdom, or any practical help for the effective achievement of a specific project, goal, or dream.

Sadly, most people seek a counselor or partner only when they are in trouble or when they have an obvious need that they can't handle by themselves. This is especially true of men. Even in a strange city, we men usually won't stop and ask for directions until we are hopelessly lost.

Solomon knew better. He would not even consider undertaking any significant endeavor without *first* seeking out wise counsel. What did he know that most of us don't? He knew that enlisting the aid of wise counselors and good partners was *critical* to achieving success, and achieving it as soon as possible. He knew that effective partnering offered tremendous benefits, and that attempting to tackle any important effort without counselors or partners was foolhardy.

◎ The Consequences of "Going It Alone"

We've all heard the comment "I did the best I could." I've heard it a thousand times, said different ways. "I can't do it any better." "This is as good as it gets." "That's not me." And "I could *never* do that." These statements may be true, in that they reflect one's personal limitations when trying to do something by oneself. However, they are also completely false; if that person were to recruit counselors or partners, they could have achieved far more than they would have thought possible. Solomon warns that doing anything without the aid of counselors or partners will radically limit one's achievement. Among the likely consequences:

Your Plans and Purposes Will Be Frustrated

In 1974, I started my own marketing consulting business. My main source of income was a single client, a commercial real estate developer. Seven months later, I lost his account when his company filed for bankruptcy. I had saved enough money to last about four months. I had two marketing projects that I thought offered a real chance to make a lot of money, but I could afford to pursue only one. In the first month, I researched and wrote out plans for both ideas. I sought one man's counsel on one of the ideas. When he told me it would never work, I quickly abandoned that idea for the other. I poured every dollar I had into the development of the other project, which was a shopper's guide to new home developments in the Phoenix area. I sought no counsel for this idea and did not try to recruit any partners. As hard as I tried, as much money, time, and effort as I put into it, I ran out of money before I could market-test the idea. I was totally broke. So broke, in fact, that families from my church began to anonymously leave bags of groceries on my doorstep, because I didn't have enough money to buy food for my wife and three-year-old daughter.

In Proverbs 15:22, Solomon tells us that without counsel, your purposes, plans, goals, or work will be frustrated, disappointed, or completely stopped. In my case, all of the above took place. No one begins a project, whether personal or professional, thinking that they are going to fail. Yet 70 percent of all new businesses fail within their first year of operation. Every couple enters marriage truly believing that they are going to live "happily ever after." Yet over 50 percent end in divorce. But the failure rates in business and in marriage are cut by *two-thirds* when counselors are brought into the equation, *before* the business is started or the marriage vows are exchanged.

You Will Fall

Have you ever suffered a fall? Nobody ever *plans* to fall—it just happens. I once stepped on some unseen ice and my feet flew out beneath me. As I was falling, I remembered the terrible feeling of panic, of being totally out of control. I remember hoping that some cushioned part of my body would hit the ground first, before my head. But I had no chance of controlling how I landed. Fortunately, my hands hit the ground first, breaking my fall. My head hit next. Both of my wrists were sprained, and I had a golf-ball-sized lump on my head, but that was it. Dr. Robert Atkins, famed creator of the Atkins Diet, wasn't so fortunate. As he walked down the steps of his home, I'm sure he had no idea that he was one step away from the last step of his life. He never saw the ice that caused his fall. Upon landing, his head bore the full impact. Despite the valiant efforts of some of New York's finest doctors, he never regained consciousness, and he died a few days later.

Solomon tells us in Proverbs 11:14 that without the aid of counsel, you will fall. The terrifying aspects of a fall are: You never see it coming, you lose all control, and you suffer injury to one degree or another. The same is true here. Solomon says that, without seeking counsel or partners, sooner or later you will fall. It's not a matter of if, but when. Said another way, don't seek counsel in your work—you will fail; don't seek counsel in your marriage—you will fall; don't seek counsel in your parenting—you will falter; and don't seek counsel in your finances—you will fail.

You Will Experience Financial Loss and Personal Humiliation

Poverty and shame shall be to him that refuses instruction.
                                             —Proverbs 13:18

Three times in my life I have had investment opportunities that seemed like "can't miss" moneymakers. I was so confident that they were "sure things" that I refused to listen to my financial counselors and made the investments against their advice. I forgot what Solomon warned in Proverbs 13:18—that the person who refuses instruction or counsel will experience both poverty and shame. Each of these three times, I lost every penny I had in savings. Each time, I was driven to the edge of bankruptcy. Each time, I was humiliated in front of my family and friends. Fortunately, my own business was such a productive partnership and so undeservedly blessed that I was always able to recover and gain back most of my losses.

A friend of mine who lost his restaurant business wasn't so fortunate. He pursued his objectives without heeding the counsel of others. He lost everything he owned. Worse, he left town without communicating with many of his investors and fled the state in shame. Both he and I could have avoided our financial losses and humiliation had we only humbled ourselves and heeded the counsel of others.

⚈⚈ The Rewards of Effective Partnering

You Will Accomplish Your Dreams, Goals, Plans, and Objectives

> *Every purpose is established by counsel . . .*   —*Proverbs 20:18*

According to Solomon, by recruiting and effectively utilizing a number of counselors or partners in important endeavors, you will achieve your goals in life. In fact, effective partnering is more than just a component in the achievement of our goals— it is *the* component that is responsible for such achievement.

After failing miserably in both of my own businesses and in six of my seven jobs, on job number ten I partnered with my mentor, who later brought in a handful of other partners. The result was radically different. We created dozens of companies, achieving billions of dollars in sales and tens of millions of dollars in personal income. It's impossible to overestimate the power of effective counsel and partnering.

You'll Reduce Your Risk

> *Where no counsel is, the people fall: but in the multitude of counselors there is safety.*   —*Proverbs 11:14*

Simply seeking a single opinion is not enough to avoid a fall. Solomon claims that if we truly want to be sure we're making the best decision possible on an important issue or concern, we need many counselors. One of my dear neighbors was told by our local doctors that she had terminal cancer and had only six months to live. They told her to get her affairs in order. When she told that to one of her friends in

Texas, he flew her to Houston to be examined by several specialists there. They embarked on a course of treatment that saved her life. Today, nearly a decade later, she is cancer-free, and the most active (and loving) seventy-four-year-old I know.

I have seen the same results in business. I have eight partners. In 1996, we were on the verge of bankruptcy due to marketing mistakes we made in 1995. We had only enough money to take on one more project. When we first tested it, the test-market results weren't sufficient for us to roll out the program into a national campaign. Of the eight partners, one, Dave Marsh, had two ideas that turned everything around. Dave's two ideas literally transformed a million-dollar loser into a billion-dollar winner. If I had only had seven partners, without Dave, our company would have gone broke. Our multitude of partners not only provided safety, it resulted in tens of millions of dollars in profits in the years that followed. In Proverbs 24:6, Solomon tells us, "For by wise counsel thou shalt make thy war; and in a multitude of counselors there is safety."

Solomon is literally talking about war here, but his recommendation is applicable to any action or competition. By seeking wise counsel before you initiate action, you are far more likely to choose your battles wisely, and win the battles you choose. So often we create conflict with our spouses, children, or others over issues that are insignificant. Objective counselors will often help us see such issues in their proper perspective. And when a conflict is warranted, they will help us approach the conflict and engage in it in a way that produces the best possible outcome. Solomon, of course, is one of the best counselors one could have. In Chapter 9, you'll learn his counsel for winning and resolving conflict.

You'll Gain Wisdom That Will Serve You the Rest of Your Life

He that walks with wise men shall be wise. . . .

—*Proverbs 13:20*

I was twenty-four years old when I met Bob Marsh and twenty-five when I met Gary Smalley. They are the wisest men I have known. Fortunately for me, both became counselors, partners, and mentors to me. As you know, it was Gary who introduced me to the Book of Proverbs. His wise counsel has helped me in dealing with personal and professional issues. Bob Marsh has been like a second father to me. He taught me more about marketing and business in three months than I had learned in four years of business school and six years in business. Both Gary and Bob's wise counsel have not only helped me at the times they were given, their wisdom remains with me. A day does not go by that I don't draw upon that wisdom.

In Troubled Times, You'll Have Someone to Help You Out

Two are better than one because they have a good return for their labor. For if either of them falls, the one will lift up his companion. —*Ecclesiastes 4:9–10*

Nobody sails through life without experiencing trials and unexpected falls. Sooner or later, they come to all of us.

Solomon states what should be obvious to all and yet seems to be missed by most—that with a good partner there will always be someone to come to your aid and pick you up. Without a partner, what would have been a temporary setback can become a permanent failure.

You'll be Able to Win Battles That Would Otherwise Be Lost

Though one may be overpowered, two can defend themselves. A cord of three strands is not quickly broken.

—Ecclesiastes 4:12

From 1979 until 1985, my partners and I created a number of television marketing campaigns for a small life insurance company. We created a joint venture in which we advanced the money for the television marketing campaign, and the insurance company provided the insurance policies to the viewers who responded. Our agreement stated that the profits from these campaigns would be split between us, fifty-fifty. In 1985, that company was purchased by a foreign company that refused to pay us our share of the profits. Their attitude was "sue us." They knew that we did not have the money to survive five to ten years of litigation. We were devastated. Not only did the company not pay us the profits they owed, they did not reimburse us for the millions of dollars we had spent on our previous campaign. We had used our credit to purchase airtime from hundreds of television stations, and now we had no money to pay our bills.

Fortunately for us, as this was happening, we brought in a

seventh partner, a brilliant former president of an insurance company and a man of the highest integrity. Without even being asked, he volunteered to empty his personal savings account and pay the stations enough money to keep them temporarily satisfied. He then miraculously negotiated a wonderful deal for us with another insurance company. We then created a campaign that made enough money to pay off all of our debt, return his money, and sustain our business. In our case, a cord of eight strands kept us from being overpowered and broken. We went on to create many new companies and overpower our competition, and for a number of years we became more productive than any public company in the world. Without the strength of partnership, we would have been overpowered and bankrupted twenty-two years ago.

You'll Achieve Greater Success

Solomon assures us that whatever success you might achieve by yourself, with the right partner you'll achieve a level of success that is wildly better! Most people pursue their most cherished dreams alone. Why? Because they don't see how much better things could be with the right partner.

In my first five years after college, I worked for eight different employers. In all these jobs, I was "on my own." None lasted very long, and my work on those jobs was never much above mediocre. My income never topped $1,000 a month. On job number nine, I recruited the help of a part-time mentor. My salary jumped to $1,500 a month, and together we doubled the company's sales, from $30 million a year to $60 million a year. On job ten, I entered a full-time partnership with my mentor; within a year, we added four more partners.

Did Solomon's promise of a "wildly better return" on our labor come true? Job ten has lasted twenty-nine years, and my income has skyrocketed from $1,000 a month to as high as $600,000 a month. Does that qualify for a "wildly better" return on our labor?

"Wait a minute," you say. "You and your partners obviously brought a lot of experience and skill to the table." Nothing could be further from the truth. I was a 27-year-old corporate failure who had never created a single successful television commercial or marketing campaign in my life. Our mentor was a 52-year-old entrepreneur who was on the verge of going out of business. The other partners were a 27-year-old dog trainer, a 24-year-old oil field worker, a 24-year-old printing estimator, and a 19-year-old convenience store clerk. Though I was the only college graduate in the group, I had experienced more failures than the rest of the group combined. Where in this group do you see the potential for building dozens of multimillion-dollar companies with billions of dollars in sales? The answer is, you don't, because that potential didn't exist among us as individuals. Rather, it was the partnership that gave us that potential. That's the incredible power of partnering.

WARNING: Take Care to Avoid the Wrong Partners

Whenever I speak to audiences about the incalculable rewards of partnering, inevitably someone will approach me afterward with a horror story about a partnership gone wrong. They usually present their experience as an argument *against* partnering. But Solomon never said partner with just anyone. Rather, he cautions, partner only with people who meet the right qualifications: "Confidence in an unfaithful man in time of trouble is like a broken tooth, and a foot out of joint" (Proverbs 25:19).

While he was visiting a remote village in Uruguay, my neighbor's son broke a tooth when he bit down on a rock that was hidden in a plate of beans. This young man is a linebacker on his college football team and has experienced a lot of pain in his years of playing football. But he told me that he has never experienced pain that can compare to what he felt when he broke his tooth. As bad as that is, imagine having a dislocated foot. Every step would be filled with excruciating pain. In both cases, the pain would be so intense that it would make it impossible to perform any work productively.

These two scenarios reflect the kind of experience you can expect if you pick the wrong kind of partner. The wrong kind of partner in marriage or in business can make your life miserable. Picking the wrong partner in any area of our life can produce life-altering consequences. Solomon offers seven red flags to watch out for when choosing a partner or counselor:

1. A lack of integrity

Whoever is partner with a thief hates his own soul.

—Proverbs 29:24

Solomon means more than a person who literally steals another person's possessions. To Solomon, a thief is anyone whose character subordinates, suppresses, or abandons honesty for the sake of self-gratification or the pursuit of ambition. A man who lies on his income tax return, cheats on his wife, or does personal business on company time is just as much a thief as one who snatches a purse, steals a car, or robs a bank. The only difference is the target and degree of dishonesty. A man who is dishonest with others will sooner or later be dishonest with you or your clients. Everyone has lied or cheated more than once in their life. But most people feel guilty about it, and their action usually represents an exception in their life rather than a norm. These are not the people Solomon warns about. He is warning about people who are quick to rationalize or excuse their own dishonesty, people for whom dishonest behavior is the rule rather than the exception. To partner with such a person will ultimately cause us to compromise our very being.

Character does count. Integrity should be the most important trait we look for when choosing a partner, a mate, or a counselor. The marriage of one of my best friends was destroyed by an unscrupulous marriage counselor. This counselor condoned his wife's extramarital affair, rather than criticizing it. My friend's wife left him for the other man, who later abandoned her when she wanted a commitment. My friend, his children, and his ex-wife paid a terrible price for choosing a counselor without integrity or wisdom.

2. A quick temper or deep-seated anger

Make no friendship with an angry man; and with a furious man thou shalt not go. —Proverbs 22:24

How many divorces would be avoided if people paid attention to this one admonition of Solomon? Dr. Gary

Smalley states that anger is the single most destructive force in a relationship. Everyone occasionally loses his or her temper. But Solomon's talking about a man or woman whose character is permeated with anger. Such people are quick to lose their temper because the root causes of their anger have never been effectively dealt with. In Chapter 11, we will look at Solomon's powerful insights regarding anger. Here we are simply warned not to form any bond or partnership with an angry person. An angry person will set aside reason, personal responsibility, and matters of conscience under the driving force of their anger. Sooner or later, their anger will bring them down and their partners will take the fall with them.

This admonition doesn't mean that you can't be kind or outgoing to such a person. It merely warns us not to enter any kind of interdependent relationship with them.

3. Foolishness

> **Leave the presence of a fool, Or you will not discern words of knowledge.**   —*Proverbs 14:7*

Solomon tells us that if we seek wise counsel and partner with wise people, we will gain wisdom that will serve us in the near term and throughout our life. The opposite is also true. If we partner with the kind of person Solomon calls a fool, we will lose the ability to discern true knowledge. In other words, we won't be able to tell the difference between good ideas and bad. Having read hundreds of biographies and business "case histories," I never cease to be amazed at how many business executives do incredibly stupid things. Seemingly brilliant men make terrible choices and errors in judgment, both personally and in their business decisions. Often these foolish decisions result from their association with foolish men, sometimes other corporate executives, sometimes consultants, and sometimes friends.

4. Anyone who offers a lot for a little

Every community is full of people who offer "opportunities" that promise a huge return for just a little investment or effort, opportunities that at first hearing sound too good to be true. Solomon warns us not to follow these people or their recommendations. And if we shouldn't follow them, then we certainly should not become involved in any kind of committed relationship or partnership with them. In Proverbs 28, he warns us that to do so can take us "into poverty." I ignored this warning and borrowed millions of dollars to invest with a person offering such an opportunity. My money was going to be tied up for only three to six months and was going to more than quadruple when the company went public. That was eight years ago. The company went bankrupt, and my millions were lost.

But you don't have to be a millionaire to get sucked into get-rich-quick schemes. Television fast-buck artists show you how to make fortunes in real estate, stock trading, and so on; all you have to do is send them a few hundred dollars to learn how. People and opportunities that ask you for very little and promise you a lot in return are people not to be trusted. When you run into them, turn around and run away.

5. The excessive use of flattery

A man that flatters his neighbor spreads a net for his feet.

—*Proverbs 29:5*

A lying tongue hates those it crushes, and a flattering mouth works ruin.   —*Proverbs 26:28*

What's the difference between praise and flattery? The Hebrew word for praise Solomon translates as "commend," while the word he uses for flattery is synonymous with "smooth talk." Flattery is "smooth talk" that is meant to puff up your ego; praise is meant to commend you for your character traits and your worthwhile efforts and deeds. Anytime a "smooth talker" flatters you, be on guard. The man who offered me the opportunity to quadruple my money only the week before had openly flattered me in front of a large audience. While my wife reacted very negatively to his flattery, my ego was puffed up. He spread his net, and my bank account was promptly emptied. I was saddled with a debt that nearly ruined me.

6. An inclination to gossip and exaggerate

He that goes about as a talebearer reveals secrets: therefore meddle not with him that flatters with his lips.

—*Proverbs 20:19*

Solomon distrusted big talkers, people who talk a lot and perform little. He had an even greater problem with liars, gossips, "flatterers," and people who reveal other people's secrets. He urges us to pay attention to what comes out of other people's mouths. When you encounter these traits in a person, do not follow their lead, do not seek their counsel, and do not partner with them. On two different occasions, before reading Proverbs, I hired assistants who turned out to be gossips, big talkers, and flatterers. One stole thousands of dollars' worth of products from our company and misrepresented her position to others outside of our company, while the other used her company credit card to make personal purchases of over a hundred thousand dollars and paid the company only half of that back. O, that I had known these Proverbs *before* I hired these people.

7. A disregard for rules, regulations, laws, or personal boundaries

> **Whoso keepeth the law is a wise son: but he that is a companion of riotous men shameth his father.**   —*Proverbs 28:7*

Have you ever known anyone who thinks or acts as if they're above the law, or who feels regulations and rules are meant for other people rather than them? Although this trait may seem harmless, it is not. People who exhibit such traits are able to excuse or rationalize anything they do. They are often high achievers. It is easy to become so enthralled by their résumés and accomplishments that we ignore or excuse these traits. Solomon warns us not to enter a committed relationship or partnership of any kind with such people no matter how successful they are. Their disregard for authority, rules, and laws will make it easy for them to excuse improper or abusive behavior toward you, your employees, or your customers.

How to pick the right counselors and partners, and avoid the wrong ones

The benefits of seeking counsel and effective partnering are so enormous, and the consequences of choosing the wrong counselors and partners can be so destructive, that it is critical that we seek the right counselors and partners for any important pursuit in our lives. Here are a number of recommendations on how to do so.

1. Use the seven red flags provided by Solomon as yardsticks by which all potential counselors, advisers, or partners should be measured. Eliminate anyone for whom any of these red flags appear.

2. When specifically looking for counselors and advisers, examine their "walk" before you listen to their talk. In the area for which they are providing counsel, what do their lives tell you? For example, why would anyone seek marriage counsel from a therapist who has not succeeded in achieving a happy marriage himself? As basic as this concept is, millions of people follow the counsel of those who have failed miserably in their own businesses or marriages. Do your due diligence. It's YOUR life they may be messing with.

3. Assess your own strengths and weaknesses. What you usually *don't* need is a partner who is a carbon copy of yourself.

4. Identify the talents, abilities, and strengths that you need in a partner or counselor to compensate for the areas of your weaknesses, inabilities, and lack of know-how.

5. When possible, look for a person who shares the same vision you have for your dreams, goals, project, or venture. Your partner not only needs to see it, he needs to identify with it and be captivated by it.

6. In business situations, look for a partner who is willing to be totally committed to your vision of achieving success. If you are totally committed and your partner isn't, I can promise you that the partnership won't last long. Look at how he has performed in other situations. Are his commitments short-lived—or faithful until the end?

7. Is your potential partner a positive person or not? People who are generally negative tend to be very poor partners. A partner doesn't have to be as positive or as optimistic as you, but if he is quick to tear down others or find the negative in situations, he's likely to jump ship when the going gets tough, or worse, steer the ship in the wrong direction.

8. Look at your potential partner's natural drives and gifts. Is he or she a talker or a doer? How do you know? Look at what they have personally done, not just what they have had others do.

Whatever degree of success you achieve in your personal or professional life, rest assured that seeking counsel and effectively partnering will increase your success exponentially. I would rather go through a dozen bad partners to find one great partner than not have a partner at all. By using Solomon's advice, you should be able to avoid the wrong ones and seek out and enlist the right ones.

Knowledge to Wisdom

STRATEGIES AND TIPS FOR IDENTIFYING
AND RECRUITING MENTORS

One of the most important types of partners we can recruit is a mentor. A mentor is someone who has already achieved extraordinary success in the area in which we want to achieve success, whether personal or professional. Here is a list of tips and strategies that many have found to be helpful in their pursuit.

1. Determine the specific dream or area of your life for which you want a mentor. Do you need a mentor to help you in your profession in general, or to help you in a particular area of your job, career, or profession (e.g., managerial skills or marketing skills)?

2. Create a list of potential mentors for each area you've decided on. Make a list of the people you respect most who might be able to give you insight, wisdom, and advice for each area in your life you want to improve. List the names in order of preference. In other words, the person at the top of each list should be the person you would choose if you could pick anyone you wanted.

3. Starting with the mentors at the top of your list, write down the status of your current relationship with each one (boss, friend, acquaintance, friend of a friend, total stranger, and so forth).

4. **Write down everything you know about that person through either personal experience with them or through second- or thirdhand knowledge.**

5. **Research everything you can about your potential mentors.** What are their likes, their dislikes, their passions? How do they spend their time on and off the job? What motivates them?

6. **If they're mere acquaintances or strangers to you, do you know anyone they know?** If you do, find out all you can from that person. Consider using that person as a reference to make your initial contact with a potential mentor.

7. **Prepare to contact a potential mentor on the phone, or in writing with a brief proposal or request.** Whether you plan to make your contact in person, on the phone, or in a letter, you need to prepare your proposal or request well before you make the contact. If you are contacting someone who knows your reference but doesn't know you, your reference should be mentioned in your opening sentence. Next, touch on the quality or qualities that you so admire about this person. Briefly explain why those qualities are so important to you and how you want to gain this person's insight and wisdom in making those qualities a part of your life. Ask if the person could spare a brief amount of time each week or month (a lunch, a breakfast, a coffee break, a round of golf) in which you could ask questions that might help you grow in this particular area.

8. Make the contact. Nothing beats a personal appointment. Depending upon your potential mentor, that strategy may or may not be practical. If you can't make an appointment to see him or her, the next-best thing is a phone call. Use a letter only when you have failed to get a meeting or make the contact by phone. Regardless of how you make contact, make it brief and to the point. Any mentor worth his salt (unless he's retired) already has a very busy schedule, and if he thinks future contacts with you are going to take too much of his time, he will either turn your proposal down outright or avoid you like the plague.

9. Follow up. After you've made your first contact, follow up with a brief note of appreciation, commenting on something specific that he or she said or did.

10. Go to the next person on the list. If your first choice for a mentor turns you down, find out why. Then go through this same procedure with the next person on your list.

CHAPTER 7

The Happiness Secret

A joyful heart is good medicine:
but a broken spirit dries the bones.

—PROVERBS 17:22

◉◉ What Do You Want?

Nearly 3,000 years ago, Solomon wrote what medical researchers have only recently discovered, that being truly happy produces wonderful health benefits. Today's studies show a reduced risk of heart disease, cancer, and susceptibility to other illnesses. On the other hand, new studies report that people who are unhappy or depressed experience a higher rate of inflammation in the circulatory system, which is a major contributor to heart disease, heart attacks, and strokes. Overall, depressed people have about twice the death rate per age category as people who are happy (that statistic does not include suicides). Research has also shown that happy people recover from illness and surgery much faster than unhappy people do.

So what will it take to make you happy?

If you could have any one thing in life, absolutely anything, what would it be? Prosperity? A better body? Good health? A long life? A great marriage? A better job? A fabulous career? What?

If you answer, "Prosperity," I might respond, "What good is prosperity without health?" If you answer, "Great health," I could point out a lot of healthy people who are miserable because they hate their jobs or don't make enough money. No matter which answer you choose, I could point out someone who has exactly what you want and yet is unhappy. Howard Hughes had it all: money, power, fame, and romance. And yet he was miserable.

The truth is, more money, better looks, better health, a better job, a better marriage, and even a longer life are really only a means to an end. What you really want goes one level deeper than that. What you really want is happiness.

HAPPINESS is a heartfelt joy that is consistent, persistent, and lasting.

---

๑๑ What Keeps Us from Being Truly Happy?

In his early years, before his wisdom was supplanted with arrogance, Solomon discovered the source of happiness—what it takes to gain it, sustain it, and grow it. He also discovered a number of major barriers that prevent most people from ever attaining it.

Looking for happiness in the wrong places

He who loves money will not be satisfied with money, nor he who loves abundance with its income. This too is vanity.

—Ecclesiastes 4:10

As Solomon's wealth grew, so did his arrogance, and he set aside his wisdom and the values that he knew to be right. He set himself on a course of trying anything and everything he wanted, from hedonism to horticulture. And toward the end of his life, he concluded that it was all an exercise in what he called *vanity*. Vanity is that which looks marvelous on the surface but, when examined more closely, turns out to be of little worth. At the end of Solomon's life, he concluded that acquiring anything that lacks eternal purpose or value was empty in its power to provide true happiness. No matter what material things a person acquires, they soon lose their appeal, and the temporary happiness they provided subsides.

A lack of gratefulness

"You don't understand my circumstances," I often hear from people justifying why they are unhappy.

Solomon suggests that no matter what reasons you have to be ungrateful, there are even more and better reasons to be grateful. In Proverbs 20:12, he points out that our eyes and ears should be appreciated as the incredible gifts that they are. You may ask, "What does that have to do with being grateful?" Everything! I work in television, and I can tell you that no camera has ever been invented that begins to compare to the human eye, and no sound system has ever been created that compares to the human ear. Like every other part of our body, they are amazing. Solomon implies that we don't have to go any further than a simple consideration of our bodies to be grateful. No man-made pump can compare to our heart, no computer can compare to our brain, and they are not a given—there are plenty of people whose eyes, ears, and hearts do not function as they should. We should be grateful for a wealth of things in our lives and days that we take completely for granted.

It's impossible to be grateful and unhappy at the same moment in time. Any moment, hour, day, or week that you are unhappy, you have chosen to let your focus rest on something other than the gifts you have been given. Let your unhappiness serve as an alarm to redirect your focus and energy. If you want to increase your happiness, follow Solomon's example: Make a list of all the things that you should be grateful for. Then, every time you notice unhappiness creeping into your thoughts, redirect your focus to those wonderful gifts.

Envy

> *Wrath is cruel, and anger is outrageous; but who is able to stand before envy?* —*Proverbs 27:4*

"If I had what he [or she] has, then I'd be happy." We've all had such thoughts. When I lived in an apartment and had little money, I envied families who had a house and more money than I. When I bought my first house, I envied people who had bigger and nicer houses. When I drove a 1961

Studebaker, I envied those who drove newer and nicer cars. When I was unhappy in my marriage, I envied friends who had happy marriages. It seemed that no matter what I gained or acquired, there were always others I envied. I became a multimillionaire with a job that I loved and a family that I adored, yet there were times I found myself envying a high school classmate who became a famous director and billionaire. Then one day I reread Solomon's words on envy. He said envy was more destructive than anger. It is impossible to be happy and envious at the same time. I either had to find a way to deal with my envy, or I would never be consistently happy. Why? Envy takes your eyes off what you have and focuses your attention on what you *don't* have. It reflects an attitude of arrogance and entitlement. When you are envious, misery and ultimately depression reign supreme.

The seeds of envy reside in everyone's heart and mind. They need to be dealt with daily. Martin Luther once said, "You can't stop a bird from landing on your head, but you can stop him from building a nest on it." We cannot prevent envious thoughts from entering our hearts, but we can keep them from taking root. And the antidote is gratefulness. Gratefulness literally means to be full of gratitude. When your heart is full of gratitude, there is no room for envy to grow.

A sense of entitlement

Every man's way is right in his own eyes . . . —Proverbs 21:2

Today, no matter what people have or what they've been given, they often feel that they are entitled to more. Husbands feel they are entitled to more than their wives provide, and vice versa. Employees feel entitled to more than they are receiving from their employers. People feel they're entitled to more from insurance companies, health care providers, and government agencies. How often do you complain because you're not getting everything you think you're entitled to from one or more people in your life? Here's a law of life we all should be aware of: As long as our heart is focused upon what we don't have and on what we think we're entitled to, we will not be happy!

Foolishness

> *He that trusts in his own heart is a fool, But whoever walks wisely will be delivered.* —*Proverbs 28:26*

The final obstacle that stands as a roadblock to happiness is our own unwillingness to look outside ourselves. We rely solely upon *our* understanding, in *our* own heart, and make our decisions based upon *our* feelings. Solomon said in Proverbs 28:26, "He that trusts in his own heart is a fool." Why? Because our feelings are not only unreliable, they can change in a moment. Our feelings are subject to an emotional roller coaster. One moment we are happy, the next we're sad or depressed. One moment we're filled with love, the next we're driven by anger. One moment we're full of confidence, the next we're filled with fear and worry. The person who trusts solely in his own heart is ultimately betting his future upon his own finite knowledge and the whims of his feelings. No wonder Solomon calls this foolishness.

∞ Overcoming the Barriers to Personal Happiness

Overcoming the barriers to personal happiness is simply a matter of doing what the various Proverbs we've read about advise us to do. Nonetheless, I thought it might be helpful to summarize Solomon's advice:

Develop a grateful heart.

This simply means that throughout each day, focus on those things for which you are grateful. For those who are currently having a hard time overcoming a devastating setback or sorrow, Gary Smalley teaches a wonderful technique called "treasure hunting" in the opening chapters of his book *Making Love Last Forever.* Applying this simple skill will help you discover hidden treasures in even your most traumatic experiences. Once you discover those treasures, nothing will stand in your way of gaining a grateful heart.

Eliminate your sense of entitlement.

A false sense of entitlement in any area of your life is an enemy that will keep you bound to unhappiness. The only way to break loose is to relinquish the unrealistic expectations you may have of others: the government, your employer, your friends and relatives, and your spouse and children. As you do this, you will be amazed by the results. You'll not only become a lot happier, you will gain an increased ability to love and respect others unconditionally.

Root out the weeds of envy.

When you find yourself envying what others have, remind yourself of three important facts: You don't know the whole story of the challenges in other people's lives. Everything a person owns is left behind at death. And death can take anyone at any time.

You don't know their whole story, how happy or unhappy they really are, or what they have sacrificed to acquire that which you envy. Did they sacrifice their personal lives? Make unethical or immoral choices? Did they sacrifice time with their family? Regardless of what they have, remember, when they die, they will leave it all behind. I'm only in my fifties, yet I've already seen some of those I envied pass on. They left behind their riches and their families. I would rather be broke and have more time to enjoy with my family than have billions of dollars and die prematurely.

Whenever you feel envy, let your feelings of envy serve as a signal to reset your focus on those things for which you are grateful.

Start living wisely.

Wisdom is not simply knowledge—knowing the truth about something. It's not merely something you store in your head like facts in an encyclopedia or database. Wisdom involves action. Simply stated, wisdom is the effective application of truth to your daily behavior. In Chapter 15, I discuss building a life upon a foundation of wisdom and learning.

Knowledge to Wisdom

1. Which of Solomon's barriers to happiness are currently keeping you from being consistently happy?

____ Looking for happiness in the wrong places

____ A lack of gratefulness

____ The envy of others

____ A sense of entitlement

____ Foolishness (trusting solely in your own heart or feelings)

2. Make a list of the things in your life that you should be grateful for. Start with the most obvious and the most important, but don't stop there. Keep adding to the list over the next few months. Ultimately, you'll have an incredible list that you should review every day.

CHAPTER 8

The Four Qualities
That Make You Invaluable

> Do not let kindness and truth leave you;
> Bind them around your neck, Write them on the
> tablet of your heart. So you will find favor and
> good repute in the sight of God and man.
>
> —PROVERBS 3:3–4

As you know, in my first six years after college I never held a job for more than a few months. Usually, my bosses were very considerate when they laid me off. They would tell me all of the things they liked about me, and then tell me that I was being laid off due to a variety of nonoffensive reasons. The truth is, I was laid off for one, and only one, reason: My employers did not value me as much as they valued the employees they kept. The people they valued the most, they promoted and paid the most. The people they valued the least, they ultimately let go. The same is true in personal relationships. Friends do not walk away from relationships with friends they value. Men and women do not divorce spouses whom they cherish. So the question becomes What makes a person so valuable that his employer will promote him rather than fire him? What makes a friend so valuable that many of her friends will consider her a *best* friend, one they would never want to be without? What makes a spouse so valuable that their mate will always adore them? Solomon reveals five qualities that, when developed and nurtured, will make anyone highly valued by others, both personally and professionally.

We looked at the first of these qualities in Chapter 2, that of diligence. True diligence will make a person the most valued employee in any workplace.

The focus of this chapter is the four other qualities that will make you truly valued in life. As with diligence, none of these qualities naturally reside in us fully developed. Rather, they are seeds that must be nurtured to grow.

∞ Kindness and Truth—Twenty-Carat Diamonds of Priceless Worth

My wife and I recently attended a charity event in Beverly Hills. One woman was reportedly wearing $5 million in diamond jewelry. A huge yellow diamond pendant hung around her neck, and a white diamond of similar size was mounted on a ring. Yet there are two qualities in a person that will far outshine that woman's expensive jewelry. Their value is priceless, yet is nearly always underestimated. Their attractiveness is universal, yet they are surprisingly rare. I'm speaking of the qualities of truth and kindness. In one survey, more than 80 percent of all high school seniors admitted that they had recently cheated on exams. In the workplace, behavior is not much different. From the factory floor to the corporate boardroom, honesty can be hard to come by. People assume that because dishonesty often brings short-term advantages, it does not have significant negative consequences over the long term. Nothing could be further from the truth. Ask the executives of Enron, WorldCom, and Tyco. And things don't get much better at home. About half of America's married men have admitted cheating on their wives, and more than a third of our wives have admitted cheating.

In today's instant-gratification, me-first society, kindness seems more like a leftover than an entrée. In other words, I'll take care of me first, and if I have any time or money left over, I'll give that to others.

In Proverbs 3:3–4, Solomon says, "Do not let kindness and truth leave you; Bind them around your neck, Write them on the tablet of your heart." Like a dazzling piece of jewelry, truth and kindness, Solomon says, should be so much a part of our lives that they would be the first two attributes a person notices about us. They should see them first, and often. When others think of us, the first thought that should come to their mind is our kindness and our integrity. These were the qualities I first noticed when I met Gary Smalley, a man who was to become one of my dearest friends. Both of these qualities radiated from his eyes; they were equally obvious in his words and actions. That is the "bind them around your neck" part that Solomon is talking about.

But that's only the first half of Solomon's directive. The second half is to "write them on the tablet of your heart." In other words, make them the central part of who you are and what you are about. For thirty-one years I have seen Gary's kindness and truth expressed toward me and to every member of my family. I have seen it expressed to every one of the friends whom I have introduced him to. Gary doesn't have to try to be kind and honest; they have become part of who he is. The same has been true with a number of other people in my life, including my mentor in business, Bob Marsh, and my spiritual mentors, Herb and Helen Selby. With each of these people, I noticed these qualities from our first encounter, over thirty to forty years earlier.

๑๑ The Incalculable Benefit of Making Truth and Kindness a Part of Your Life

Throughout the Book of Proverbs, Solomon makes conditional promises: "If you do this, then you'll get that." The same is true of truth and kindness. If we make them a vital part of our lives, then we will gain a benefit that no amount of money on earth can buy! He tells us in Proverbs 3 that we will receive the favor of men, women, and God, and gain good standing with them. The Hebrew word Solomon chose for "favor" translates to "cherished approval and preferential treatment." In other words, you will be cherished by friends, peers, colleagues, bosses, employees, and family. But there are other benefits as well:

They create secure and treasured relationships.

Knowing that you can rely on a trusted friend's word makes you feel safe and secure in that relationship. Honesty provides a concrete foundation upon which a lasting relationship can be securely built. Kindness creates value and appreciation in a relationship. A person who routinely extends unexpected acts of kindness makes you value that relationship above others.

They provide encouragement and build self-esteem.

When I was fired from my fourth job, Bob Marsh, the executive vice president of the parent company, took me to lunch. He asked what I was going to do, and when I told him that I had accepted a job with a bank in Arizona, he asked if I had any business suits that would be appropriate for working at a bank. When I told him that I did not, he drove me to a clothing warehouse and bought me two new business suits. As I was nearly broke, this act of kindness made a huge impression upon me. It made me feel more valued than did any other event in my business life. It raised my low self-esteem higher, and as a result, I started my job at the bank with a completely different frame of mind about myself and my self-worth.

They increase commitment, loyalty, and motivation.

Whenever you're kind to someone, it raises their level of commitment and loyalty to you. It also motivates them to follow your example by returning kindness, both to you and to others. Three years after Bob Marsh gave me those two suits, he invited me to start a new marketing company with him. At the time, I was working for a large catalog company that offered to double my salary and promote me to the position of vice president of marketing if I would stay on. So my choice was to stay with a solid company that would pay me $36,000 a year, provide me with a company car, and promote me to VP of marketing; or leave the company, move my family 2,500 miles, and become a partner with Bob in a start-up company that could afford to pay me only $10,000 a year. I knew that if the start-up company succeeded, I could make a lot more, but it was a real gamble. But the decision wasn't difficult at all. The chance to go into business with the one businessman I admired and valued more than any other was a dream come true. So I accepted his offer. Fortunately, our business succeeded beyond our wildest imagination. Bob has long since retired, but his sons and I continue to enjoy a partnership and friendship beyond description. Not only has our company prospered; more important, we have enjoyed working together every day for nearly three decades. And it all started with a single act of kindness.

◎◎ Roadblocks to Kindness and Truth

Knowing the incredible benefits to inscribing kindness and truth on the tablet of our hearts, why on earth would anyone put them aside for self-centeredness and dishonesty? The answer is simple. Our self-centeredness and self-involvement are like a mental and emotional muscle that we have been exercising daily throughout our lives. It is truly the strongest muscle we have. Its reflexes are quick and powerful. Anytime we are confronted by any situation that gives us a choice between our own interests and simple kindness, our automatic response is to act in our own accord. It will always focus our attention on what we need, want, and desire.

Kindness, on the other hand, is a mental and emotional muscle that is exercised *only* when we make a conscious choice to do so. It forces us to set aside our personal needs and desires long enough to focus our attention on the genuine needs of others. When we choose to use *this* muscle, we must overpower our reflexive self-centeredness. Every day we face countless opportunities to choose between our own self-interests and kindness. Although it is not an easy task, the more we exercise this muscle of kindness, the stronger it becomes. And the stronger it becomes, the greater a part of our inner core it becomes. Over time, we will embrace it more naturally with little conscious effort at all.

Why is it so easy to lie?

When most of us think of someone who is dishonest, we usually think of other people and rarely of ourselves. But the fact is, if one includes exaggerations, little white lies, and the conscious omission of relevant facts, most of us are guilty of dishonesty on a regular basis. Why is it so easy to exaggerate, bend the truth, or lie by omission? Because doing so temporarily puts us in a better position than telling the absolute truth would. There are only three reasons to be dishonest: to promote ourselves, to protect ourselves, or to manipulate the thoughts, feelings, or actions of others. Unfortunately, all three of these reasons are false perceptions. We think we are going to benefit when we are dishonest, but whatever gain we experience is always short-lived, and the consequences of being dishonest are long-term and ultimately outweigh the temporary gain dishonesty provided. Each time we're dishonest, we become less sensitive to our conscience in the future, and we create a greater capacity to lie next time. Sooner or later, such dishonest behavior becomes our normal daily experience. It becomes part of who we are and how we interact with the world. Moreover, for the most part others see right through us, whether they articulate that awareness or not. Dishonesty has destroyed lives, marriages, Fortune 500 companies, and even governments.

In my opinion, dishonesty comes in two forms: distorting the truth and hiding the truth. The first is obvious; the second may not be. Think of Arthur Anderson. If any firm should be honest and truthful in the corporate world, it should be the accountants and the auditors of the business community. They are charged with the responsibility of analyzing and accurately reporting the current financial conditions of a company to the public. Yet in the case of Arthur Anderson, they conspired with Enron executives to misrepresent the facts. Doing so allowed Enron's executives to continue their deceptive practices until the corporation collapsed, destroying the savings of thousands of employees and countless shareholders. One Enron executive committed suicide; others have been sentenced to prison. Anderson's reputation and business were destroyed; 28,000 Anderson employees lost their jobs. And this is just the obvious damage. Corporate America will be forever suspect by the public, viewed as organizations run by greedy executives who will do whatever it takes to line their pockets, regardless of the cost to the public.

But dishonesty never starts in a corporate boardroom. It starts in the hearts and minds of individual men and women. By making honesty the cornerstone of your personality, you can avoid such consequences.

◎◎ The Ultimate Consequences of Dishonesty That We May Not See Until It's Too Late

Dishonesty destroys the foundation of relationships with others and with God.

As we discovered in an earlier chapter, Solomon lists seven things in Proverbs 6:16-19 that he says God hates and considers "abominations." A "lying tongue" and a "false witness who utters lies" are two of the seven. I don't know about you, but I'd much rather be found doing something that brings God's favor than doing that which God hates. But God is not the only one who hates dishonesty. Nearly all women and most men say it is the single greatest turnoff in any relationship.

Dishonesty produces never-ending stress.

Why? Deep down inside, you carry a hidden fear that one day your dishonesty will be exposed. You also know you have to keep your story straight. Dishonesty forces you to always think about your past lies so you won't say anything contradictory that exposes those lies. All of this creates stress, and we've already seen that stress not only robs us of any potential for joy, it ultimately steals our health as well.

Dishonesty ultimately creates unexpected crashes.

Every year, there are a number of train wrecks, dozens of plane crashes, and millions of car accidents. And yet no one ever boards a train or plane or steps into a car thinking they're about to be in a traumatic or fatal crash. Likewise, no one ever tells a lie or hides the truth thinking that doing so is going to destroy the very life they are trying to enjoy; but it does. Sooner or later, nearly all dishonesty is discovered by others, and when it is, a crash always results.

∞ Generosity—The Quality That Receives More Than It Gives

One man gives freely, yet gains even more; another withholds unduly, but comes to poverty. A generous man will prosper; he who refreshes others will himself be refreshed.   —*Proverbs 11:24–25*

Generosity is one of the most admired attributes any person can exhibit. Whether a child donates his hard-earned allowance to a disaster-relief effort or a businessman donates millions of dollars to charity, we feel appreciation and admiration for those who are generous. But admiration and appreciation aren't the only benefits of generosity. In addition to

THE FOUR QUALITIES THAT MAKE YOU INVALUABLE   115

the heartfelt joy experienced whenever you help meet the needs of others, Solomon promises that those who are generous will never lack for anything—every true need will be provided—and that you will prosper, and your prosperity will always increase. In Proverbs 11:24–25, he tells us that those who give generously to others will gain back even more than they give. Sound impossible?

Psychologists tell us that the two greatest motivating forces in a person's life are their desire for gain and their fear of loss. Solomon assures us that generosity directly impacts both. If you could wave a magic wand that would guarantee you would never lack for your material needs, and that you would experience an ever-increasing prosperity, how much would that wand be worth? Solomon puts that wand in your hand; all you have to do is to become truly generous.

What does Solomon mean when he talks about generosity? Collectively, the words he chooses imply that a generous person is one who freely gives a significant portion of what he has to meet the needs of others, and that he does so with no expectation of receiving anything in return. Although he's speaking primarily of being generous financially and materially, generosity isn't limited to that. Being generous means being focused on meeting the genuine needs of other people, whether with money, deeds, or emotional support or assistance.

A lot of people think that you have to be rich to be generous. Nothing could be further from the truth. One of the most generous people I have known was a janitor I worked with in college. He scrubbed toilets five nights a week and took care of his bedridden wife during the day. He was generous with everything he had: his time, his kind words, his thoughtfulness, and his considerate acts. I once asked him if there was anything he needed. "Heavens no," he replied. "Everything I have ever needed has always been abundantly provided." To this day, I have never met a happier man. As Solomon promised, he never lacked anything; and just as he refreshed others, he was refreshed.

And those who are not generous? Solomon says they will fall into poverty. Not necessarily financial or material poverty, but poverty of the soul. They are never satisfied with whatever they have and constantly need more. They become emotionally bankrupt. Generosity starts in the heart. It always takes action, and it is never passive.

◉◉ Graciousness—The Attribute That Raises You Up in the Sight of Others

A gracious woman attains honor.　　—*Proverbs 11:16*

According to Solomon, the one quality that will bring you glory, honor, and an attractiveness that is best described by the word "splendor" is that of graciousness. What does Solomon mean by the word "gracious"? The Hebrew word Solomon used incorporates kindness, patience, tactfulness, elegance, appreciation, and favor. It means extending these qualities to others beyond what is expected or deserved.

Although Solomon uses this word in referring to women,

that may be because in his eyes these qualities seem to be more naturally inherent in women than men. The fact is, however, they are rare in both sexes. I spend a lot of time in airports, and when flights are delayed (as they often are) I am constantly surprised by the impatient, rude, and sometimes crass behavior that seems to be commonplace today.

The good news is that graciousness is not a personality type; it's a choice anyone can make. And the first step to becoming gracious is to choose to become grateful. Solomon would have us be grateful for everything we have, every day of our life. When we are constantly aware that every important thing we have is a gift, it is possible to be gracious to others. Being genuinely grateful creates within us a gracious spirit: The choice of being patient when you're feeling impatient. The choice to extend kindness when you are angry and feel like giving somebody what they "deserve." The choice to tactfully and gently correct someone instead of criticizing him. The choice to extend appreciation even when you don't feel like it. True graciousness does all of this without any expectation of receiving anything in return. As you develop a heart of graciousness, and extend that graciousness to others in your daily life, you will receive the honor that Solomon promises and all that it brings with it.

Knowledge to Wisdom

MAKING SOLOMON'S FOUR QUALITIES A PART OF YOUR LIFE

1. Whom do you personally know who is a living example of Solomon's four qualities? Name at least two people for each quality.

Impeccable honesty _____

Kindness _____

Generosity _____

Graciousness _____

2. Think back over the past several days. Write down specific examples of when you exaggerated, told a white lie, omitted an important fact, or told an outright lie.

3. For each of the examples in number 2 above, write out why you did so. Did you see any significant gain from the lie? Would anything significant have been lost had you simply not exaggerated or lied?

4. What can you do differently tomorrow to break the habit of exaggerating, stretching the truth, and so on?

5. Describe any situations or encounters with others this past week in which you could have extended more kindness, generosity, or graciousness.

6. Describe any situations or encounters this past week in which you were able to extend kindness, generosity, or graciousness without expecting anything in return.

CHAPTER 9

Winning and Resolving Every Conflict

> A brother offended is harder to be won
> than a strong city: and their contentions
> are like the bars of a castle.
>
> —PROVERBS 18:19

Conflict and Adversity Are an Unavoidable Part of Life

Like it or not, conflict and adversity are as much a part of life as eating, drinking, and breathing. But according to Solomon, conflict and adversity serve very important purposes in our lives that are rarely accomplished by any other means. If you deal with them correctly, they will produce positive outcomes and strengthen your relationships at work and at home. If you don't handle them correctly, they will produce negative outcomes and harm your potential for happiness and success. Trying to weather adversity or conflict without Solomon's strategies is like trying to ride a bicycle from Florida to Maine during the height of hurricane season. You might be able to do it, but not without a great deal of stress and danger. And your likelihood of failure is much greater than your likelihood of success.

◎◎ Who wins and who loses in adversity and conflict?

When Henry Ford fought with the directors of the Detroit Automobile Company over which direction the company should take (producing expensive cars for the proven market of the affluent or producing inexpensive cars for the nonexistent market of the masses), he lost the fight. He was ultimately fired. The company failed shortly thereafter, and its investors lost their investments. Henry Ford went on to create the Ford Motor Company, becoming one of the richest men in the world, and his investors in that venture saw returns on their investments of more than $3,000 for every dollar they invested. So who was the real winner of the conflict at Detroit Automobile Company? Henry Ford officially lost, and the directors and investors seemingly won. Yet in reality the opposite was true.

Walt Disney's first animation company was gutted and all but destroyed by an unscrupulous distributor who took Disney's most popular cartoon character (Oswald the Lucky Rabbit) and hired all but one of his animators away from him. Disney was devastated. The distributor thought it had won big-time. But that company later went bankrupt, while Walt Disney created an entertainment empire.

The fact is that over time the real winners of a conflict are not necessarily those who seem to be the initial winners. Similarly, adversity may ultimately spawn not just challenges but opportunities. Each time I was fired from one of the nine jobs I held after college, I was devastated. And yet had I not

lost those jobs, I would have never experienced the unimaginable success that came with the tenth. The problem for all of
us is that we cannot see into the future. As a result, we make
our judgments about adverse situations and conflicts before,
during, and immediately after the fact. Consequently, our
judgments may lead us to the wrong conclusions. Solomon
teaches us that when we see the true purpose of conflict and
adversity, we can seize the opportunity they present and can
ultimately be the winner in even the most heartbreaking circumstances.

There are two kinds of conflict and adversity. The first is
conflict and adversity that we create or contribute to. The
second is conflict and adversity that is created by others or by
circumstances outside of our influence or control. Let's look
first at conflict and adversity that is created outside of our
influence or control.

◎◎ Conflict or Adversity That Is Beyond Our Control

In Proverbs 17:3 Solomon writes, "The refining pot is for silver and the furnace for gold, but the Lord tests hearts." My
grandfather was a mining engineer in the early 1900s. When I
was in the first grade, my father came home from a visit with
his sister in a mining community in Arizona. Whenever Dad
came home from a trip, he brought my sister and me a little
surprise. On this occasion, he pulled a little bag out of his
suitcase and poured out a handful of ugly rocks onto our
kitchen table. I was tremendously disappointed. They didn't

look any different from the stones in our backyard. Then he told me what each one contained. "This one has gold in it, this one has silver, and this one has copper," he said. I asked him why they weren't shiny, and why I couldn't see the gold, silver, or copper. He replied, "They haven't been through the fire yet." He explained that they had to be placed in a very hot fire, hotter than I had ever seen; only the fire could separate the beautiful metals from the rock around it.

According to Solomon, there is an extraordinary purpose to the type of adversity or conflict that comes into our lives that is beyond our control. That purpose is to melt away the outer crust of common rock that surrounds our souls and hearts and produce, refine, and reveal the character within. Exceptional attributes emerge that cannot be developed by any other means. Like the refining process of gold or silver, the result of this is that we become much stronger emotionally, psychologically, and spiritually. Rocks containing minute quantities of gold are worth a few dollars per ton. Refined gold is worth hundreds of dollars per ounce. Similarly, conflict and adversity are the smelting processes that can create or refine our true character and all the powerful attributes that attend such character: patience, compassion, kindness, courage, faith, perseverance, loyalty, integrity, and love. So rather than being angered, discouraged, or resentful of adversity and conflict, we should embrace them for the benefits and opportunities they provide. For without the fires of adversity and conflict, there is no refining process for our character or heart.

So each time we encounter adversity, we have a choice to make. Either we can give in to it and become discouraged and angry, or we can choose to be patient and look to the long-term benefits that may result. Whether we make a conscious choice or choose by default, the choice is ours nonetheless. Choosing the first path will make us bitter and guarantee our sense of loss; choosing the latter will make us better and stronger.

However, most of the conflict and much of the adversity that we experience is a direct result of our actions. During the last twenty years of my father's life, he had heart surgery three times. At the age of seventy-nine, after a seven-month battle with lung cancer, he died. His heart surgeries and his cancer produced tremendous suffering for him and for me. But his heart disease and his cancer were fueled by his life-long habit of smoking.

When I was fired from my third job, my disloyalty to my boss was a major factor. And most of the arguments I have had with others, I either started or fueled.

⊚⊚ Conflict Makes a Dull Blade Sharp

In Proverbs 27:17, Solomon says, "Iron sharpens iron, So one man sharpens another." It is hard to cut with a dull knife. It must be sharp. Until recently, the best way to sharpen a knife was to rub it against a whetstone—a kind of flint. Doing so created friction and sparks, but as a result, the knife was sharpened. Solomon tells us that our characters are sharpened in the same way—through our close and even friction-filled interaction with others. In business, it is not uncommon for arguments to result in the discovery of an unexpected course of action that creates a breakthrough for the business. Gary Smalley teaches that conflict is the gateway to the deepest levels of communication and intimacy in a marriage or relationship. People who run away from conflict and avoid confrontation at all costs can unintentionally do more harm in their relationships than good. A marriage without conflict and confrontation will never achieve a deep level of intimacy. Conflict should be seen not as a dreaded enemy, but as a necessary tool for optimum achievement in any walk of life.

◎◎ Redefining Our Concept of Winning

Our notions of winning an argument are often simply to get the other person to agree with us and to get them to do what we want. By this definition, the directors of Detroit Automobile won when they prevailed over Henry Ford. But in reality, both sides lost. To truly win in any situation is to achieve the best possible outcome. Usually, that's what both parties really want, but their judgment may be clouded by their own biases, their desire to prevail, or their failure to see the whole picture. They argue without a full grasp of all of the facts, or strictly from their own self-centered point of view. On the other hand, when Ford convinced the investors in the Ford Motor Company to back his vision of affordable automobiles for the masses, he won, his investors won, and millions of people throughout the world won. Later, he persuaded everyone that Ford Motor Company should continue to offer consumers only one color (black) while other manufactures were offering a wide choice of colors. Even though he won the argument, he and everyone else lost. The company nearly went bankrupt. Using Solomon's communication strategies from Chapter 5, and his instructions on handling conflict that we'll look at next, we can gain a better perspective for any argument and better help all parties involved to see more clearly and pursue the best possible outcomes. Winning becomes no longer a matter of getting "my way," or persuading someone to do what I want them to do; rather, it becomes a way of achieving what's best for all.

Conflict can be beneficial or detrimental, depending on how we engage in it.

Whenever we engage in an argument, whether we initiate it or are responding to the person who did, our natural inclination is to defend ourselves and our point of view, and to attack or counterattack the other person and their point of view. In most cases, we have no other goal than that. We also have no rules of engagement. We say whatever comes to mind at the moment it comes to our mind. We shoot from the hip and usually inflict more wounds than are either necessary or beneficial. And we receive more wounds in return. Consequently, our relationship is temporarily or permanently damaged. Solomon says that this is foolishness. Regardless of what draws us into an argument, as soon as we realize what is happening we should take control of our words and change our focus. Instead of simply defending or attacking, we should shift our focus to achieving the best possible outcome for both parties. In the "Knowledge to Wisdom" section at the end of this chapter, Gary Smalley provides a list of dos and don'ts for arguing and resolving conflict that will enable us to do just that.

◎ The Causes of Hurtful Conflict

Solomon tells us that there are five causes of detrimental and destructive conflict. Whenever we consider engaging someone in an argument, we should ask ourselves if any of these causes are the basis of our conflict:

1. Pride. Proverbs 13:10 states, "Only by pride comes contention. But with the well advised there is wisdom." As we'll discover in Chapter 14, our natural arrogance or pride is the instigator of more of our problems than any other source. Solomon claims that it is the number-one source of conflict. So before you engage in conflict, ask yourself if your primary motive for pursing an argument or conflict is simply to sustain or build your ego, or defend it when it's been attacked. If it is, that's not a valid reason to start a fight or be drawn into a conflict. Solomon's suggestion? Seek advice from outside counsel *before* being drawn into a conflict. He implies that the wisdom gained from such counsel will usually allow you to refrain from engaging in a conflict driven by pride. I've seen husbands and wives attack each other over nothing, and do the same with their children. Here again, Solomon simply says don't do it. Save your arguments and conflicts for *real* issues, where genuine harm has been done or is going to be done, and a conflict is the only way to resolve or stop it. Contend with someone only when you have a real reason or cause to do so, not out of petty pride.

2. Anger. As Proverbs 15:18 says, "A hot-tempered man stirs up dissension, but a patient man calms a quarrel." Arguments are often started not because they're necessary, but because one party is angry. And more times than not, this anger has nothing to do with the argument. If you are the person harboring anger, grapple with the issues that are fueling your anger before it destroys important relationships in your life. If the other person carries around unresolved anger, avoid being drawn into a conflict with him or her, even if it means limiting the amount of time you spend with them. In Chapter 11, we'll look at Solomon's prescriptions for dealing with anger in our lives and the lives of others.

3. Harsh words. Proverbs 15:1 says, "Soft words turn away wrath, but grievous words stir up anger." All it takes to start or fuel a conflict is a single harsh statement or a few hurtful words. In most relationships, we know what buttons to push to start a fight, and we know the words and statements that will push those buttons. Pushing those buttons is not a valid motive or means for starting a fight. Solomon suggests that we take control of our mouth and use kind and gentle words to reduce tension, rather than harsh words to stir it up.

4. *Impulsive reaction.* In Proverbs 25:8, Solomon says, "Do not go out hastily to strive, lest you know not what to do in the end thereof." Most arguments are started impulsively; few are carefully thought out beforehand. Solomon warns that an argument or conflict started on impulse has a much greater likelihood of hurting you in the end, rather than helping you. His prescription? Don't do it. Stop and think about alternative courses of action.

5. *Meddling in other people's conflicts.* Proverbs 26:17 says, "He that passes by and meddles with strife belonging not to him is like someone who lifts up a dog by the ears." It's only natural to try to help others in their conflicts. But as natural as that is, Solomon says that by doing so, *you* will be the one who gets bitten. Taking one person's side against another without knowing all of the issues is a recipe for disaster. One of my best friends was deeply hurt by the actions of one of his adult sons. When I heard about it, I wanted to jump on the phone and straighten his son out. But I was wisely warned by one of our mutual friends to stay out of it unless I was asked to intervene by either the son or the father. So I did stay out of it. A few months later, the son realized his error and sought his father's forgiveness. Today their relationship is stronger than ever. Had I stepped into their conflict, it may have harmed my relationship with one or both of them in a way that may have lingered long after their conflict was resolved. Even when you are asked to intervene in someone else's conflict, do so only after a great deal of consideration and counsel. Never be afraid to decline, and to let the feuding parties know that it is really none of your business. More often than not, this is the right course of action.

⊚⊚ Solomon's Steps for Winning in Conflict and Overcoming Adversity

Armed with our revised concept of what it means to win (to achieve the best possible outcome), we are now ready to consider Solomon's advice for winning conflicts and overcoming any adverse situations.

Solomon gives eight insights for engaging in conflicts and for achieving the best possible outcome.

1. Understand the potential consequences of the conflict. In Proverbs 18:19, Solomon tells us that a brother offended is harder to be won than a strong city. He wants us to realize the consequences of engaging in an argument or conflict—they may be much worse than we're ready for. Winning back a person's friendship, trust, or commitment may be next to impossible; the contention may create an insurmountable barrier. This does not mean that we should avoid valid confrontation, only that we should carefully consider the potential consequences as a part of our decision making.

2. Keep as your goal "achieving the best possible outcome for all parties involved." Remember that the true purpose of conflict is to make things better, not worse. Our goal is to gain the best possible outcome not only for us but for all who are involved.

3. Seek counsel before engaging in a conflict. In Proverbs 20:18, Solomon tells us that "every purpose is established by counsel." Knowing our purpose in conflict is to gain the best possible outcome, he tells us that the best way to achieve that purpose is to first seek good objective advice from those not engaged in the conflict.

4. Do not answer a fool in the manner he attacks. Many arguments and conflicts are immature at best and foolish at worst. Solomon advises us not to come down to the level of our attackers. If someone calls us names or attacks our character, don't respond by calling the other person names and attacking their character. Solomon tells us, "Do not answer a fool according to his folly, lest you also be like him." He goes on: "Answer a fool as his folly deserves." Attack and expose his argument, and do not attack him personally. If he is not receptive to your input, then just walk away. Let him suffer the consequences of his foolishness.

5. Don't reveal confidential information. When we are engaged in an argument or conflict, it is natural to cite the opinions, feelings, and statements of others to strengthen our case. Often, these have been shared with us in confidence; revealing them during an argument is a violation of that confidence. It is in this context that Solomon warns us in Proverbs 25:9–10: "Do not reveal the secret of another, lest he who hears it reproach you, and the evil report about you not pass away." Violating the confidence of another in the course of an argument will do long-term damage to your reputation and relationships that you will ultimately regret.

6. Never prolong an argument. When we do engage in an argument, everyone wants to get the last word in, making one last point or throwing one last jab. Solomon urges us to resist this natural inclination. In Proverbs 15:1, he tells us that "soft answers turn away wrath, but grievous words stir up anger." By introducing a soft tone of voice, kind words, and constructive statements, we can quickly de-escalate tension and conflict. In Proverbs 26:20, we're told, "Where no wood is, there the fire goes out: so where there is no talebearer, the strife ceases." The more you fuel an argument, the bigger it gets and the more hurtful it will be. So stop gossiping and stop adding fuel to the fire.

7. Give an unexpected gift. Solomon tells us in Proverbs 21:14, "A gift in secret pacifies anger: and a reward in the bosom, strong wrath." Since reading this Proverb, I have used this tactic dozens of times, and it has worked every time. One time, one of my former partners did something so upsetting to me that I was ready to end our friendship. I thought, "This is the final straw, I don't want to have anything more to do with him." The next day, when I came into my office, there on my desk was an incredible gift wrapped with a big red bow. A card was attached to it that read simply, "I am sooooooo sorry. Please forgive me." In a moment, all my anger vanished and we were buds once again. Such a gesture doesn't always require a big gift. All it takes is an unexpected gift, given with an apology. The gift can be as simple as a short note expressing appreciation or an apology.

8. Be quick to forgive. In Proverbs 10:12 Solomon tells us,

"Hatred stirs up strife, but love covers all transgressions." Anytime someone hurts us it gives us a wonderful opportunity to respond with forgiveness, to be kind and loving. There is no act or attribute that is more pleasing to God than that of forgiveness. But it can be exercised only when we have been unjustly offended. That is why we should be truly grateful for even those people who have hurt us the most. The greater the hurt, the better the opportunity for forgiveness. The greater our forgiveness, the more godly our character becomes.

ꙮ Dealing with Adversity

Solomon gives us a number of insights that we can use when we find ourselves in adverse circumstances, regardless of their source or its degree of difficulty:

Realize that adversity is a valuable part of life. Adversity provides us with the opportunity to develop our character in a natural, recurring, and powerful way that only the challenges of adversity offer. According to Proverbs 17:3, only adversity refines and reveals the gold and silver of our character. Nobody likes going through adversity at the time we are going through it. Without going through it, our character "muscles" would never reach their full potential strength and power.

Until my father died, I do not remember feeling a genuine compassion for someone who lost a parent. When he died, I experienced sorrow like I had never known. I missed him a thousand times more than I thought I would. For the first time, I realized what other people were going through when they lost their mothers or fathers. Before, I'd just give them a pat on the back and a few superficial words of comfort. Now I can genuinely sympathize with what they are going through, and I can help them so much more.

Accept responsibility for your contribution to the situation. A lot of times adversity comes our way as a direct or indirect result of our own actions. We make a bad choice or a bad decision, or we simply fail to do something we should have done. When I made bad investment decisions, I had to accept responsibility for my greed and my naive choices. Yes, several men had misrepresented the opportunities to me, but the fact is, I am the one who made the decisions. And I experienced the very consequences that Solomon had cautioned his readers about. Anytime you make a contribution to your own adversity, you need to accept responsibility for it. Don't simply blame someone or something else.

Nonetheless, throughout our lives we will experience a great deal of adversity that is *not* a result of our actions. In those cases, it is critically important that we do not assign fault to ourselves or those who had nothing to do with it. When a friend of mine lost his daughter to leukemia, he confided to me that he felt God was punishing him for his past sins. In other words, he was blaming himself. Solomon believed that adversity sometimes has a purpose that we cannot know or understand. As tempting as it may be, to try to figure out such a mystery is not only an exercise in futility, it is foolish.

Closely examine the adversity you encounter to learn from it. Our neighbor's fifteen-year-old daughter lost her life in the tsunami that hit Thailand on December 26, 2004. Although he will never know the purpose of that event, he did gain an infinitely greater realization of the temporary nature of life. As a result, he made the decision to make the absolute most of every remaining day of his life. Because of the love and kindness he was shown by Thai villagers who had also lost family members, he is more actively helping the helpless himself. When Hurricane Katrina ravaged the Gulf Coast, he instantly and effectively campaigned for help from our community.

Seek insights from other people. A lot of times, adversity blindsides us. So what do you do? This is exactly the kind of situation in which Solomon would advise us to seek outside counsel. Go to others and gather their insights. What went wrong? Why didn't I see it coming? Was I blind? Was I callous? Was I naive? Others can sometimes see what we cannot because of our closeness to the situation.

ൟ The Best Way to Navigate Through Adversity

Whenever we encounter adversity, our natural inclination is to panic, cower, surrender, or retreat. Solomon tells us that there is a better way, namely, face it head-on. In Proverbs 28:1, he tells us, "The wicked flee when no man pursues him, but the righteous are as bold as a lion." In other words, when adversity comes, this is no time for timidity. As Solomon says,

"If you faint in the day of adversity, your strength is small." For those who *don't* faint, and instead hang in there, their strength of character will grow. Perseverance is critical to achieving extraordinary success and fulfillment. But it cannot be developed without adversity. Solomon tells us that "a just man falls seven times and rises up again." Each time we get up after a fall, we are exercising perseverance, a quality and strength that will then serve us well throughout our lives.

∞ The Benefits of Adversity

In conclusion, there are two benefits we receive from adversity that cannot be acquired through any other means. First, you develop qualities of patience, strength, courage, compassion, kindness, love, humility, and faith. Second, you become infinitely more valuable to others when *they* experience adversity. The people best equipped to help others through adversity are those who have already gone through it.

Knowledge to Wisdom

GARY SMALLEY'S RULES OF ENGAGEMENT: THE DOS AND DON'TS OF CONSTRUCTIVE CONFLICT

CONFLICT DON'TS

Don't bury the problem or the pain it's causing you. Don't think that the answer to any conflict is to avoid it, or to bury the problem with denial. If you do, that hurt will grow like an untreated infection and create even greater problems in the future.

Don't let a confrontation degenerate into an attack on the other person's character. Stay focused upon the problem. Don't dilute your argument by focusing on the other person's weaknesses or character.

Don't use inflammatory remarks, sarcasms, or name-calling. Don't generalize or exaggerate. When you use any of these in an argument, it completely changes the focus of the argument, causing the other person to defend him- or herself, or make excuses, drawing their attention away from the real issue. It will also make them deaf to anything else you say.

Don't enter a conflict with condescension or the attitude of a know-it-all. To achieve the best possible outcome, enter any conflict with the spirit of a learner—one who also has weaknesses and problems. This can be especially hard for bosses, spouses, and parents to do, but it's a must to treat the other person with the same respect you would expect or desire of them.

Don't let the conflict broaden to other issues. Regardless of the temptation to bring up other issues, keep your argument focused on the issue causing the conflict.

Never use ultimatums or threats. When you use ultimatums or threats, you are backing the other person into a corner. That may force a destructive counterattack on their part. It also changes the focus from the issue at hand and instead makes the threat or ultimatum the focus.

Don't use disrespectful body language or demeaning nonverbal communication. Rolling your eyes, shaking your head, slapping your forehead, or using that popular retort "Duuuhh" is both rude and demeaning.

Don't interrupt. Let the person say what he or she wants to say. Let them get it all out. Stay focused on what they're saying. Nod to show your attention. Show patience. Control your tongue. This will show that you value the other person, and because you've listened carefully to their concerns, it will make them much more receptive to your genuine concerns and thoughts.

Don't raise your voice. Remember that soft words turn away anger but harsh words stir it up. Keep your tone of voice respectful.

Never walk away, or withdraw, or hang up the telephone in the middle of a confrontation. Remember, the best way to get another person to really hear what you're saying is to show honor and respect during the communication. Withdrawing, walking away, or hanging up on the other person shows the opposite. The only time it's appropriate to hang up or walk away is if the other person starts to become verbally or emotionally abusive.

CONFLICT DOS

Take a time-out to regain your emotional control. Wait until you are calm before you engage in a confrontation.

Prepare for the confrontation before you engage in it. Rather than acting hastily and shooting from the hip, take time to determine your specific goal for the confrontation. Do you simply want to resolve a current problem? Do you want to stop a behavior pattern, or do you want to attempt to replace a destructive behavior pattern with a more constructive one? Do you want to correct, encourage, or punish? You should want the confrontation to accomplish a specific goal, not just to inflame an already bad situation. Write down your goal if time permits. Determine how to begin the confrontation in the least inflammatory way.

If your intent is to give criticism, use the sandwich method. Deliver your slice of criticism sandwiched between two slices of praise. Start by stating a positive attribute about the person, then deliver the criticism, then end with more positive statements.

Use as many encouraging and positive statements as you can in the context surrounding the issue you're trying to address or resolve. Your goal is not to tear down the other person, but rather to constructively address and resolve a problem. Adding encouragement and praise to your argument helps them to know that your goal is to help rather than to hurt. It makes it easier for them to listen, understand, and respond in a positive way.

Be willing to offer and accept a progressive resolution of the problem or issue. In other words, don't expect the problem to be resolved instantly. Be willing to work at it with a person. Realize that *time* is often the most important ingredient for lasting change.

Ask for advice on what you can do to help resolve the problem. This not only shows humility on your part, it shows a sincere willingness to take responsibility for any contribution your actions have made to the problem. It also shows that you want to attack the problem as a team, rather than as two adversaries.

If the person attacks you, don't retaliate. Instead, when they attack, urge them to tell you everything. Ask them, "What else do I do that offends you?" Assure them that you, too, have weaknesses that you need to work on. This will prove that your real desire is to achieve the best possible outcome.

When possible, reassure the person of your ongoing commitment to them and your desire to strengthen and build the relationship. Let them know that your commitment to them and to your relationship is the reason you want to address this conflict or problem.

CHAPTER 10

Turning Your Worst Enemy into Your Best Friend

He that refuses instruction hates himself:
but he who listens to reproof acquires understanding.

—PROVERBS 15:32

At that PBS television appearance I mentioned earlier, I asked the studio audience, "How many of you like being criticized?" Not one hand was raised. I then asked, "How many of you *hate* being criticized?" This time, nearly every person in the studio raised a hand. Finally I asked, "How many of you can remember a criticism you received in your childhood from a parent, a teacher, a friend, or someone else that *really* hurt you?" Almost instantly, nearly every person raised a hand again. Even audience members in their late seventies could recall hurtful criticisms from their youth. That's how terribly painful criticism can be. Most people today hate criticism and treat it as a dreaded enemy. They do everything they can to avoid it, and when it comes, they defend against it, rationalize it, run away from it, or attack the critic.

Like everyone else, I, too, used to hate criticism. And yet it seemed that my life was full of it. It came from anyone and

143

everyone: my friends, my bosses, and even my wife. I tried to deal with it in all of the normal ways: ignore it, run away from it, deny it, defend, argue, make excuses, and, more often than not, shift the blame toward someone else or attack the critic.

୭୭ Better Than Secret Love

In studying the Book of Proverbs, I discovered that these reactions can be far more destructive than the criticisms themselves. Solomon's unique view of criticism is revealed in Proverbs 27:5. Instead of reacting to it as an enemy, he says we should respond to it as a secret lover. "Open rebuke is better than secret love." Think about that. Can you remember how you felt when you first fell in love? Remember getting a love note from your sweetheart? The anticipation you felt as you watched the clock slowly tick off the minutes until your next date? Can you remember how you felt the first time he or she took your hand or gave you that first kiss? As good as that was, Solomon claims criticism is even better.

As I read this proverb, I thought, "What on earth does Solomon mean?" And yet I decided to take his advice and give it a try. The next time someone criticized me, I embraced that criticism rather than reacting against it. For several days, I had been working on a script for my first major television commercial. The moment I finished, I ran it over to my boss's house to let him read it. As he started to read the commercial, I expected to see him smile. Instead, I saw him grimace. He looked up at me and said disappointedly, "It's pretty good, but there's no hook." I was devastated. Instead of receiving a high five, I was given a criticism. But at that moment, I remembered Solomon's advice and made a decision to treat my boss's criticism as a secret lover. Instead of arguing the case for my script, I embraced his criticism and simply asked, "What do you mean, 'a hook'?" He explained what a hook was and why it was critical to always include one right at the top of a commercial. After a couple of minutes, I wrote a new opening line and read it to him. This time his reaction was completely different. With a giant grin on his face, he looked up and said, "Now, *that's* a hook!"

That commercial launched our company, producing sales of a million dollars a week. By embracing my boss's criticism, I not only changed the way I wrote that commercial—I made sure I put a strong hook at the beginning of every television commercial I wrote. During the past twenty-nine years, my commercials have produced billions of dollars in sales for our company.

Now let me ask you a question. If a stranger walked up to you and gave you a check for millions of dollars, would you treat him like an enemy or a friend? My boss's criticism was such a stranger. Solomon wasn't nuts after all. In fact, learning the right way to deal with criticism has made everything in my personal and professional life far better than I could have ever dreamed possible.

๑๑ How Do You Deal with Criticism?

If you are like most of us, you probably react to criticism in one or more of the wrong ways. Do you instantly defend yourself or your actions? Go on the offensive and attack the critic? Quickly shift the blame and point a finger at someone else's failings? Do you go into denial, either by making excuses or running away from criticism by withdrawing physically or emotionally from the person criticizing you? If any of these describe your normal reaction to criticism, don't feel bad. These are *natural* reactions. But our natural reaction is the wrong way to deal with criticism. And turning our back on it can have devastating consequences.

ꙮ The Consequences of Reacting Negatively to Criticism

Unhappiness, lack of fulfillment, and worse. In Proverbs 15:32, Solomon writes, "He that refuses instruction hates himself, but he who listens to reproof acquires understanding." *Reproof,* of course, is synonymous with criticism. The Hebrew word for *instruction* means "chastening," or disciplinary instruction. In today's vernacular, we could call it *constructive* criticism. So Solomon is telling us that the person who can't take constructive criticism is severely hurting himself. He then contrasts that with a person who listens and correctly responds to reproof or criticism, saying they will increase their level of understanding.

Solomon gives one of his gravest warnings to those who cannot accept criticism in the very first chapter of Proverbs: "They would not accept my counsel, they rejected all my reproof. So they shall eat of the fruit of their own way, and be filled with their own devises. For the waywardness of the naive shall kill them and the complacency of fools shall destroy them." In other words, when you reject counsel and criticism, you *will* get your own way, but your way will ultimately lead to your undoing.

Problems that can't be fixed. In Proverbs 10:17, Solomon says that the person who heeds correction or constructive criticism will stay on the path of a fulfilling and productive life, but the person who refuses (ignores or forsakes) reproof will stray off of that path. Look at the face of any clock or watch and notice the slight angle between two minutes—for example, between 12:00 and 12:01. That tiny angle is only three degrees. Yet if a space shuttle is launched at the moon and veers off its path by a three-degree angle (a fraction of an inch), it will miss the moon by more than 13,000 miles. When we wrongly react to criticism, we will stray off the path to a fulfilling life, according to Solomon. Though it may be only a tiny deviation initially, over a lifetime or career the consequences can be devastating. In Proverbs 29:1, he warns, "A man who remains stiff-necked after many rebukes will suddenly be destroyed—without remedy." I've seen this Proverb proven over and over again in individual lives, marriages, parent-child relationships, and in the corporate world.

Poverty and shame. In Proverbs 13:18, Solomon warns, "Poverty and shame [will come] to him who neglects discipline, But he who regards reproof will be honored." My business partners, my financial advisers, and my wife all gave constructive criticisms warning me not to invest in one particular financial venture. I refused to listen to their warnings and criticisms and invested millions of dollars in what I believed was a "can't-miss" opportunity. It missed, and I lost everything. And all of this was witnessed by the people who meant the most to me—my family, my business partners, and my trusted financial advisers. To say I was shamed is an understatement.

Stupidity. Solomon sums up the consequences of refusing criticism with a single word in Proverbs 12:1—"He who hates reproof is stupid." There have been a number of times in my life where I have covered my ears with my hands and ignored the criticisms of others. I ran full speed ahead on my own course, oblivious to everyone's warnings. In each case, the results were catastrophic. When I look back, the only word that adequately describes how I acted and how I felt is "stupid." And I'll bet everyone who witnessed these debacles would have described my actions with the same word.

The Good News . . .

Imagine that you're sick and your doctor prescribes a new medication for your illness. He says he wants to see you back in the office in three days. If, when you return, he looks worried and says your body is "reacting" to the medication, you have cause to be nervous. On the other hand, if he smiles and says your body is "responding" wonderfully to the medicine, you feel relief. That is a simple illustration of the difference between reacting and responding. *Reacting* against criticism can bring life-altering negative consequences into our lives. But correctly *responding* to it can bring tremendous benefits.

☙ Here's What You Can Expect When You Respond Correctly to Criticism

A more productive and fulfilling life. In Proverbs 10:17, Solomon tells us that the person who responds to criticism will stay on the right pathway to a full life.

Understanding and wisdom. According to Proverbs 15:32, the person who listens and responds to criticism acquires understanding. When you acquire it, you own it and experience all of its benefits for life! And in Proverbs 15:31 and 29:15, we are told that listening to reproof will bring us wisdom. How valuable are true understanding and wisdom? The richest man who ever lived tells us throughout the Book of Proverbs that these two qualities are more valuable than silver, gold, jewels, or any amount of money.

Greater joy. Again, Solomon viewed criticism as better than a first love. In Proverbs 27:9, he tells us that hearty counsel brings more joy to our heart than a healing ointment or a rich perfume. Later, he says that a wise critic is better than a beautiful piece of fine jewelry to those who would embrace and follow the critic's advice.

Honor. In Proverbs 13:18, Solomon tells us that the person who correctly responds to criticism will receive honor in his or her life. And that is something that money can't buy. At a recent piano recital, my nine-year-old son played the title song of *Phantom of the Opera*. He played this six-page piece with passion and without the benefit of sheet music. This was at a recital where even the teenagers played much easier pieces. When he finished, the parent of one of the other participants looked over at me with her mouth wide open in awe. My son was honored with enthusiastic applause from the audience. What the audience did not see was all of the coaching and constructive criticism my son had received from his teacher during the weeks of lessons that prepared him for that recital.

Sharpness. I've traveled millions of miles on thousands of airline flights during my career. In all of that traveling, many of the people I've sat next to have been ordinary, some have been interesting, and a few have been extraordinarily sharp. By that, I mean they've impressed me with their intelligence, how quick they were on the "uptake," and their sharp wit. When a person is extremely sharp, their value to any business is apparent the moment they open their mouth.

The sharpening process is loud, it's grueling, and both the sharpener and the one being sharpened take a lot of heat. My best friends in life are also my best critics, and throughout my life they have made me sharp. Going through the process is never easy. But the ultimate outcome always makes the process worth the sparks. In Proverbs 27:6, Solomon tells us, "Faithful are the wounds of a friend." In other words, it's better to receive quality criticism from a friend than a pat on the back from somebody who really doesn't care about you. When we respond correctly to the criticisms of a friend, they will ultimately build us up, making us better equipped to handle anything life throws at us.

∞ The Right Way to Respond to Criticism

Over the years, I have found that there's only one right way to respond to criticism. The good news is that when you respond to it properly, it loses all its power to hurt you.

Turning any criticism from a dreaded enemy into a valued ally involves three steps. First, carefully consider the source. Second, determine the accuracy of the criticism. Finally, you must change your behavior or actions in response to criticism you have judged to be true.

Consider the source.

Is the person offering criticism qualified by their own knowledge and experience to make the judgment they have rendered? Is their perspective complete and accurate, or incomplete and distorted?

When my third boss fired me, he said, "You will never succeed in marketing." But he really wasn't qualified to make that kind of forecast. Yes, he was a marketing expert, but he wasn't a prophet or a fortune-teller. Often, criticism is given by people who are not adequately qualified to give it. When you realize that, you can brush off that criticism as invalid.

On the other hand, when my boss on job number ten said of my first commercial, "There's no hook," he was more than qualified to make that criticism.

Consider the accuracy of the criticism.

When my third boss told me, "You are the single greatest disappointment in my entire career," I was initially flattened by the remark. But that night I considered the accuracy of his criticism. There was no way that I could have been the biggest disappointment in his career—I just wasn't that important to him. He was the senior vice president of marketing of a huge corporation. I was only an assistant product manager, a very low-level position. I'm sure that in his long career in marketing he had experienced many disappointments that were much greater than a junior manager's subpar nine-month performance.

When I realized that his remark was a gross exaggeration, it was no longer nearly as painful. I realized he was deliberately exaggerating in order to hurt me. As you consider most of the criticisms that come your way, you'll find that many are inaccurate.

Take criticism under advisement and determine the appropriate response.

The final step is the most important. It starts when you choose not to instantly react to the criticism, but rather to take it "under consideration." This will give you the time to analyze the criticism, consider the source and its accuracy, and then determine your best response to it.

There's a beach near San Diego that in the morning sparkles with what appear to be trillions of tiny flakes of gold. While lying on the beach trying to get a little sun, my young sons thought it would be funny to grab a bucket of water and give me a shocking surprise. Receiving criticism is a lot like getting an unexpected bucket of that water thrown in your face. First, although it may be a shock, there's nothing dangerous or incapacitating about having a bucket of cold water thrown into your face. Likewise, criticism usually blind-sides us and shocks us.

But we don't have to run away or attack the critic. The words are only water. Grab a towel and wipe off your face. The water in criticism is the invalid part—the exaggerations, superlatives, and generalizations. However, like the bucket of water my kids threw, criticism always contains a little sand that gets into your eyes. It stings, blurs your vision, and takes your attention away from everything around you. You want to get it out of your eyes as fast as you can.

The good news is, sand is easily washed out. And when it is, you can refocus your attention on the important things around you. With criticism, the sand is the stinging part—the spirit of the critic, his anger, the harshness of his words, the implications of his criticism, and even his motive for criticizing you. The best way to wash *this* sand out of your eyes is to write down exactly what the critic said. Later, read it, without seeing their body language or hearing their tone of voice. Often, this will take away the hurtful emotional part of the criticism that we are so quick to react against.

Next, consider the motive of the critic. If their goal was simply to hurt you, then you might need to reconsider your relationship with them in the future. However, most of the time, the motive of the critic is to correct us, protect us, or point us in a direction that they believe is for our own good. When that's the case, understanding their motive softens the sting and helps you receive it far more objectively. The fact is, whether their motive is to help you or hurt you, when we take the next and last step in this process, it is impossible for their criticism to hurt you. Even if they have the worst of motives, you can use their criticism to bring about long-term benefits in your life.

Mining for gold.

In every bucket of criticism that's thrown at us, there is always a little gold. It may be the tiniest of flakes, or it may be a giant nugget. When my boss told me that my commercial needed a hook, that criticism turned out to contain an entire bank vault full of gold. On the other hand, when my third boss fired me, I had to go through that bucket with a magnifying glass to find the gold in his criticism. When he told me I was the single greatest disappointment in his entire career, I had to ask why he was so angry at me. Why would he say such mean things to a twenty-three-year-old kid? Looking back over the nine months I worked for him, I realized I had become bored with the monotonous routine of the job. So I moonlighted, doing outside projects for other divisions of the company. He viewed this as disloyalty. *That* was the underlying reason for his anger and criticism. I decided that in my future jobs I would go out of my way to show loyalty to my bosses and refrain from moonlighting. This really paid off in a big way. Though my ex-boss's intent had been to hurt me, his criticism provided an essential building block for my future. If you mine the criticisms you receive, no matter how hurtful or devastating they may be, you, too, will find nuggets of gold that can forever change and improve your life.

❦ The Right Way to Offer Criticism

Whether you are a boss, a spouse, or a parent, you should not go out of your way to criticize others. Most of the criticism we give to others is unnecessary. Some can be extremely hurtful and create bigger problems than they solve. We should be quick to receive criticism and very slow and thoughtful in giving it. Solomon warns us that we have the power to wound or break a person's spirit with our criticism. It can literally change the course of their lives. In Proverbs 18:14, Solomon says, "The spirit of a man will sustain his infirmity, but a wounded spirit who can bear?" In other words, a man or woman can usually find the strength to deal with a physical injury or illness. But Solomon says that a wounded spirit can be truly unbearable.

This being said, *constructive* criticism is a very important and necessary part of life. Even though it should be offered sparingly, it should be given whenever it is truly needed. But there are hundreds of ways to wrongly criticize someone, and only one way to criticize correctly. First, we should not criticize when we are angry. Remember, the only valid purpose for criticizing anyone is to bring about positive change. So if you're angry, take a time-out and wait until you've cooled off. Then determine what you want to say and the best way to say it. In fact, many of the "Dos and Don'ts of Conflict" at the end of the last chapter apply equally to giving criticism and receiving it.

Gary Smalley suggests a method of criticizing that I have used for years, and it nearly always brings about positive results. Gary calls it "the sandwich method." Every sandwich has a slice of bread on each side, and a yummy middle, whether it's meat, fish, poultry, or peanut butter. With criticism, each "slice of bread" should be praise or a positive statement.

So before you focus on the meat of the criticism, lay down a slice of praise or encouragement. Honor the other person with your tone of voice, gentle words, and eye contact.

Then make the transition to the meat of the criticism. You tell them what they are doing or have done wrong or imperfectly, and suggest how they can improve. As you give them direction, ask for their input. Let them see from your demeanor and your words that you are on their side, and that your goal is to achieve the absolute best for them.

After you've finished with the meat of a criticism, add the final slice of encouragement, specific praise, or a pat on the back.

Warning: Solomon says there are some people you should never criticize.

The whole purpose of criticism is to help someone. Solomon warns us not to criticize a person who will only ignore, reject, or react against your criticism. He writes, "Do not reprove a scoffer, lest he hate you," and later adds, "Whoever corrects a mocker invites insult; whoever rebukes a wicked man incurs abuse." We all know people like this. If we reprove them, they will hate us, insult us, or even abuse us. It's better to let such people experience the ultimate reproofs of life. Solomon says in Proverbs 23:9, "Do not speak in the hearing of a fool, For he will despise the wisdom of your words."

Knowledge to Wisdom

The best way to begin to change habits is to first review experiences from your past and mentally apply what you've learned. This will enable you to effectively change your habit of reacting to criticism to one of responding to it. It will also help you more effectively help others with constructive criticism.

Receiving Criticism

1. Make a list of some the more memorable criticisms that you have received at home or at work.

2. Next to each of the criticisms you listed, determine how qualified the person was to give such a criticism. Write a V for very qualified, an S for somewhat qualified, and an N for not qualified at all.

3. Beside each criticism write down as many of the following reasons that may have been the basis of the person's criticism:

- E　Based on *emotions*
- PE　Based on your or their *past experiences* or past failures
- LU　Based on their *lack of understanding* or fully comprehending your goal, intent, or vision
- CT　Based on their *conventional thinking* rather than creative thinking
- L　Based on *logic*
- RS　Based on the *realities of the situation*

4. What was the motive of the critic? Was it their concern for you or the project and their genuine concern for others? Or was it selfishness, jealousy, fear, animosity, hurt or anger, or their own immaturity?

5. Looking back, how accurate was their criticism?

    A. Define the "water" in the criticism—that which was exaggerated, absurd, or meaningless.

    B. Define the "sand" in the criticism—that which was most irritating or hurtful (specific words, tone of voice, spirit of criticism, etc.).

    C. Determine the "gold" in the criticism—the truths that can be drawn from the criticism that can help you better perform in the future.

6. How did you respond to the criticism? With anger, defensiveness, denial, blame, attack, or withdrawal? Or did you listen, acknowledge, thank, or give the critic an explanation that helped them to better understand you or your action?

7. How could you have responded in a way that would have been better for you, your growth, and your relationship with the person offering the criticism?

8. Write down the best ways you believe you could respond to criticism in the future.

GIVING CRITICISM

1. Are you quick to criticize, or slow? (Ask family members, friends, and coworkers.)

2. Do you thoughtfully prepare your criticisms, or simply react to situations and "shoot from the hip"?

3. Do you criticize from the point of view of someone who thinks they are better than the other person, or with the spirit of a helper?

4. Do the people you criticize feel better after the criticism, or worse?

5. List some of the recent criticisms you have leveled at others. If you can't think of any, ask your spouse, children, parents, siblings, or coworkers. (If they can't remember any, you're already a saint.)

6. Next to each criticism, describe how you delivered it, how it was received, and the ultimate result in the life of the person you criticized.

7. Describe how you could have turned each criticism into a more positive experience.

8. Write out an example of how you could have delivered a criticism using the sandwich method.

CHAPTER 11

Overcoming the Most Destructive Force in Relationships

Wrath is cruel and anger is outrageous.

—PROVERBS 27:4A

Recently, my community was shocked by the news of a senseless killing of a 23-year-old woman. She was sitting in her parked car with her older sister and her three-year-old daughter, when her ex-boyfriend approached her. They started to argue, and he became so enraged that he pulled out a sawed-off shotgun and killed her with a single shot. This morning I read of a father who was so angered by his daughter's suspension from her high school softball team that he took a baseball bat and beat up her coach.

Although these examples may appear to be the extreme exception, similar events take place every day. Less severe expressions of anger, with devastating consequences, happen in thousands of relationships every day. A young friend of mine, married only four months, asked her husband what she thought was an innocent question. He exploded in anger and, in a moment of rage, pinned her to the ground with his knee on her throat. Her husband had no record of violent behavior. He was a successful medical doctor and a Sunday-school teacher.

None of the men mentioned above started their day thinking they would do something terrible that would radically change their lives. The ex-boyfriend had simply planned to ask his ex-girlfriend to give him the car they had once shared. The father had planned to ask the coach to reinstate his daughter to the team. And the husband of my young friend had simply come home from work planning to have a normal evening with his new bride.

Why do millions of people make foolish decisions that end up costing them everything they value? Solomon knew the answer. Like millions of others, they had never learned how to deal with anger. As Solomon says in Proverbs 14:17, "A quick-tempered man acts foolishly."

Left unchecked, anger can destroy your personal happiness for a moment or for a lifetime. It can destroy relationships at home and at work. In fact, marriage expert Dr. Gary Smalley says that anger is the number-one cause of divorce and the destruction of personal relationships of all kinds.

◎ The Power of Anger

Wrath is fierce and anger is a flood. —*Proverbs 27:4a*

Solomon describes the destructive power of anger as a downpour or a flood—"outrageous and overwhelming." Have you ever been caught by an unexpected downpour? Last year I was driving on a highway when one opened up out of nowhere. With my windshield wipers at their highest speed, I couldn't see five feet in front of the car. I had to pull off the road and wait it out. A senior at our high school wasn't so fortunate. Her car hydroplaned and hit a concrete wall, killing her instantly.

Floods are even more "overwhelming." They can destroy whatever is in their paths: roads, bridges, buildings, and lives. This is the true nature of anger. It can start like a light rain and turn into an extreme downpour. Like a tsunami wave, it can seemingly come out of nowhere and overwhelm anything in its way. What about *your* temper? You may think, "Yeah, I have a temper, but it's no big deal." But the fact is, even a little temper can, in a moment, turn into a downpour or a flood, causing you to lose control.

How do you feel when someone close to you lashes out in anger? Whether your response is to run away or fight, being the target of someone else's anger is unsettling at best. No one wants to be close to someone who is angry. And how do you feel when *you* are angry at someone else? Are you able to go about your day in a calm frame of mind, or does your anger fester, creeping into your thoughts and feelings? Most people don't enjoy being angry any more than they enjoy being the focus of someone else's anger.

◎◎ The Consequences of Anger

Anger creates contention. Solomon says, "A wrathful man stirs up strife." If there's a lot of conflict in your life, there's a good chance it's not the result of other people's behavior. You may have anger that has never been effectively dealt with.

Anger drives others away from us. Solomon tells us, "Do not make friends with a hot-tempered man, do not associate with one easily angered." Everyone's natural inclination is to get away from an angry person. But when their temper tantrum is over, our inclination is to rationalize it and resume the relationship. Solomon advises us not to associate with someone who is full of unresolved anger. Think about it— every year thousands are killed and millions more are physically abused by spouses, boyfriends, and girlfriends who have never extinguished the anger that resides in their hearts.

Anger lowers our self-esteem and the self-esteem of others. Solomon says, "He that is soon angry deals foolishly." Have you ever done anything that has made you or those around you feel foolish? A quick-tempered person acts foolishly because anger distorts his or her vision and perspective. It can distort our view of situations and our ability to see a person's words or actions in true perspective. Consequently, we overreact rather than effectively respond to the reality of a situation.

◎ The Rewards of Controlling Your Temper

You will have the power to overcome contention and strife. In Proverbs 15:18, Solomon claims that "he that is slow to anger appeases strife." Controlling your temper allows you to maintain objectivity, even in the midst of an argument or fight. Not only will your demeanor be a calming influence on the argument, your clear and accurate perception of the situation will enable you to provide solutions that those who are angry cannot see.

You will have greater understanding. As Solomon says, "He who is slow to anger has great understanding, but he who is quick-tempered exalts folly." Because your perception is neither blurred nor blinded by anger, your understanding of the realities of a situation increases.

Your accomplishments will increase. In Proverbs 16:32, Solomon writes, "He who is slow to anger is better than the mighty, And he who rules his spirit [is mightier] than he who captures a city." In our culture, where so many are not in control of their emotions, those who maintain that control have a tremendous advantage. They will not only enjoy greater success in the workplace, they are much more likely to have happy relationships at home as well.

You will be more highly respected by others. "The discretion of a man defers his anger, and it is to his glory to pass over a transgression," writes Solomon. My son Ryan is a running back on his football team. At a recent game, an opposing player threw an intentional late hit on him. The referee saw it and threw a flag. As Ryan got back up, I noticed that he was grimacing in pain. About five minutes later, the other team had the ball and Ryan was playing defensive end. This time, he made a diving tackle against the same player who had made the late hit on him. As the player was lying on the ground, I saw Ryan bend down and ask him if he was okay.

After the player caught his breath, Ryan reached out a hand and helped him back up. During the season, Ryan had made lots of first downs and touchdowns, but that moment made me more proud of him than anything else he achieved that season. Ryan's action was the very picture of Solomon's advice on "passing over a transgression."

◎◎ How to Effectively Deal with Your Anger and the Anger of Others

Is there anything we can do to reduce anger's power over us? Is there anything we can do to reduce our *inclination* to become angry? Is there anything we can do to *defuse* anger in other people?

◎◎ The Root Causes of Anger

According to Dr. Gary Smalley, anger is not a primary emotion. It's a secondary emotion caused by unresolved hurt, frustration, fear, or a combination of these. When we become angry, we can deal with its true source, in which case it will soon dissipate. Or we can react to the situation or other person by expressing our anger, or retain it and store it up. Most people do the last two. Expressing anger creates the negative consequences we've already looked at, hurting others and ourselves in the process. Storing up our anger or burying it isn't any better. It produces resentment and bitterness, and will ultimately poison our thoughts. Sooner or later we will not be able to hold our resentment back any longer, and from that point forward we will find ourselves with an explosive temper that can be triggered by even tiny irritations.

The only way to resolve anger effectively is to treat its root causes. We have to deal with the emotional hurts, frustrations, and fears that come our way on a regular basis. How do we do that? As Gary Smalley suggests, dealing with each of these is simple but not easy. It's simple because each of these emotions has a single root cause: our unfulfilled expectations.

At birth, 100 percent of our needs are met by other people. As we progress through childhood, other people continue to meet most of our needs. Even in adolescence, we expect others to meet many of our needs. As a result, we gain an unrealistic sense of entitlement. That sense of entitlement can become a major roadblock to our happiness. It creates a set of expectations that we place on others. We expect that other people will do things that will make us happy and fulfilled. We expect them to do those things that show that they value and appreciate us. In every relationship we have, we subconsciously build a list of expectations. We expect others to do positive things and to refrain from doing negative things. Whenever anyone fails to meet our expectations—or even worse, do something that is contrary to our expectations—frustration and hurt result. And the longer a person goes without meeting an expectation, the more we fear that that expectation will never be met. These unresolved hurts, frustrations, and fears go on to create the secondary emotion of anger.

How can you effectively deal with your expectations? First, identify them. Anytime you feel hurt, frustrated, or fearful, ask yourself what expectations you had that have been neglected or rejected. Once you've identified them, you have a choice. You can clench your emotional fist around that expectation and hold on tight, or you can mentally open your hand and release it. Our inclination is always to hold on to it, but doing so will only cause the hurt, frustration, or fear to continue to fester, creating anger, resentment, and bitterness. Or you can choose to release it, letting go and moving on with life. By releasing that expectation, you gain a peace of mind and a freedom from anger.

⊗ Eliminating Unresolved Anger

Gary Smalley says we all carry an "anger cup" in our hearts containing our stored-up reserve of liquid anger. For some people, their cup is full to the brim. It may be filled with a lifetime of anger, or maybe just a day's worth. Dropping even the tiniest amount of irritation into the cup will cause the anger to overflow and spill onto whoever created the irritation. The most insignificant event—somebody cuts them off on the freeway, or ignores or rejects a single expectation—can set off the person with the full cup of anger. It may be expressed with a temper tantrum, emotional withdrawal, backbiting, or an outright physical attack. Or it may be bottled up inside, poisoning the recipient with bitter, cynical, hateful, or depressed thoughts and feelings.

On the other hand, some people have anger cups that are 90 percent empty. They can experience irritations and unfulfilled expectations without causing an overflow. What about yours? Is it filled to the brim? Three-quarters full? Or nearly empty? Regardless of how much anger is stored up in your anger cup, it's important to focus on what you can do to drain it out completely—and keep it empty.

In his video series *Hidden Keys to Loving Relationships,* Dr. Smalley reveals seven steps that we can follow to drain the anger stored up inside us. These steps can be used anytime you find yourself angry for any reason. Taking these steps will keep your anger cup empty and prevent resentment and bitterness from poisoning your personality. This is what Solomon means when he talks about "deferring anger."

☙ Gary Smalley's Steps to Removing Anger

Define the offense in writing. When we are offended, it's often because somebody has either reduced our potential for gain or increased our potential for loss. We feel violated. Write down specifically what that person did and what it took away from you. Has it created a permanent loss, or was it a loss that diminished with time? Did it affect your self-esteem? Did it hurt your feelings? In the heat of the moment, our emotions can blow things out of proportion. When you write down how someone has offended you, you will often see it in a more realistic perspective.

Allow yourself to grieve the loss. Sometimes a terrible loss has been inflicted. I had trusted one individual to conservatively invest my life savings. Instead, he took tremendous risks, lied about the losses, and in a few months he had lost 95 percent of my savings. Needless to say, I was angry. After my father died, I had less patience with my children, my wife, and my employees, and I didn't know why. I later figured out that I was harboring anger over the loss of my dad. In each situation, Gary Smalley reminded me to write down my loss and allow myself time to grieve. When we don't allow ourselves the time to grieve the loss, the unresolved hurt can create a reservoir of anger in us.

Try to gain a better understanding of the offender. Why did the offending person say or do the things that have hurt you? Did they know that they hurt you, or were they blind to it? Did they simply treat you the way they treat everybody else, or perhaps the way they are treated by others? What is their frame of reference? Are they simply immature? Everyone has blind spots, and often they inflict hurts on others without intending the damage they have caused. When you realize that a person has done something that was a function of their personality, their immaturity, or their ignorance, the pain is not nearly as great. For years, my wife, Shannon, was deeply hurt by the actions of one of her friends. When she discovered that her friend treated everyone that way, and that it was a function of her background and personality rather than an intent to hurt her, Shannon was freed from the anger that had built up in her heart.

"Treasure-hunt" the offense. Look for the good that has come out of that situation. Has it made you more compassionate toward others? Has it motivated you not to treat others the way that person has treated you? A friend of mine lost a child in a hit-and-run accident. Prior to that, he had never set foot in a children's hospital. He could watch news reports of similar events and never feel a twinge of sadness or compassion. After he lost his daughter, he became one of the most compassionate men I've known. He routinely visited his local children's hospital to offer empathy and comfort to the parents of sick and injured children.

A pearl is created by the irritation of a grain of sand. When we experience conflict, adversity, irritations, or offenses, they often create hidden pearls. Recognizing these pearls can replace with gratefulness the hurt and anger you initially felt.

Write a letter (but don't mail it). Why? Because your anger, resentment, and bitterness will be released through your pen or keyboard. But the release is in *writing* the letter, not sending it. You need to be as honest and descriptive as you can be. Don't hold back. The purpose is to get everything out, and self-editing will only defeat that purpose.

Release the other person from the hurts they have inflicted and from future expectations. Solomon tells us that overlooking a transgression is to a person's glory. The Hebrew word for "overlook" means to set aside and go beyond. The Hebrew word for "forgiveness" means "to release." To truly forgive someone, you must release them from their responsibility for the hurt they have caused you. Forgiveness isn't a feeling or a word; it's a *choice*. And Solomon says that when you make that choice, you will receive glory. By releasing the other person, and releasing any future expectations you have of them, *you* will be released from your anger and bitterness.

Reach out. When there is no physical danger or potential for harm, reaching out to the offender with kindness and understanding can be of tremendous benefit to both of you. Let me give you an example. My partner Jim had a terrible relationship with his father. Throughout Jim's childhood, his dad was physically abusive to him, his brother, and his mother. The abuse was both severe and habitual. Even as an adult, Jim hated his father. Gary Smalley helped Jim go through the seven-step process described here. The hardest part of the process came the day Jim had to reach out to his dad. Miraculously, the day he reached out, he and his dad started a whole new relationship. It not only removed a lifetime of anger in Jim's heart, it completely changed his father's life as well. They became best friends and had an incredible relationship for the last twenty years of his dad's life.

∞ Dealing with the Anger of Others

In dealing with other people's anger toward us, we're really talking about two different situations: reducing their anger in a particular circumstance, and helping them to reduce the reservoir of anger in their heart. Here are Solomon's suggestions for reducing anger in a situation in which tempers are flaring.

Return softness for harshness. "A soft answer turns away wrath. But grievous words stir up anger," says Solomon.

Instead of returning insult for insult, try responding with a softer tone of voice and kind or gracious statements. More often than not, the other person's anger will subside.

Don't add fuel to the fire. Solomon writes, "For lack of wood, the fire goes out." So many times we want to have the last word. When we do, it's like throwing another log, or even gasoline, on the fire. We can remove fuel from the fire by accepting responsibility (or the other person's blame) for the things we did or said that were hurtful, rather than simply excusing or defending our words or behavior.

◎◎ How Can You Undo the Damage Caused by Your Anger?

Anytime you lose your temper with someone else, you have inflicted a blow. If they are more mature than you, they may have dealt rightly with it. But more often than not, the pain is not easily forgotten, and you need to take responsibility to undo the damage you have caused. Doing this involves the same process we use to remove the anger from our own heart, but with a little different spin. In addition to the steps for removing anger from your own heart that I discussed earlier, you should:

Define your offense toward the other person. What have you done that inflicted the hurt? How have you rejected or ignored their expectations? How have you created a loss or diminished a gain? Clearly define the nature and degree of your offense. (Don't justify it, excuse it, minimize it, or rationalize it.)

Tell the other person how sorry you are. Talk specifically about the particulars of your offense. Nobody appreciates or believes a generic apology. An apology that states the specifics shows the other person that you really understand what you did and how it hurt them.

Ask for forgiveness. Again, be specific about what you would like the other person to forgive you for.

Work to restore the relationship to its earlier state. Let the other person know that you wish to respect their boundaries and move at *their* pace.

True wisdom is never passive; it is always proactive. Solomon offers specific suggestions we can use to deliver us from hurts, frustrations, unfulfilled expectations, and anger. It comes when we treat those who offend us in a way that runs totally contrary to the natural inclinations of human nature.

Never seek revenge. In Proverbs 24:29, Solomon writes, "Do not say, 'I'll do to him as he has done to me; I'll pay that man back for what he did.'" He warns against revenge in any form, from talking back to paybacks. As Proverbs 26:27 says, "Whoever digs a pit shall fall therein. And he that rolls a stone it will return unto him."

Never gloat when a person who has hurt you gets hurt. In Proverbs 24:17, Solomon says, "Do not rejoice when your enemy falls and do not let your heart be glad when he stumbles."

Look for opportunities to do good to those who hurt you. As Solomon writes in Proverbs 25:21, "If your enemy is hungry, give him bread to eat. If he is thirsty, give him water to drink." Yes, this is contrary to human nature. Yet, when we help those who have offended us, we not only take fuel from their anger, we show them that we are as concerned about others as we are for ourselves.

‿ Resolving Anger Isn't a Single Victory

Anger is an emotional force we need to deal with over and over again throughout our lives. The good news is, we don't have to be victimized by our anger or anyone else's. Anger starts like a light rain—a drop here and there. Left unattended, it can become the flood that Solomon warns of. But you can take steps to make sure that it doesn't overpower you or undermine your relationships. You can keep your cup of anger bone dry.

Knowledge to Wisdom
HOW FULL IS YOUR ANGER CUP?

1. Are you easily hurt, irritated, or frustrated by "little things"?

2. Do you find yourself irritated or frustrated rarely? Somewhat often? Or nearly every day?

3. Are there any grudges or resentments you're currently holding on to in your relationships? Are there any people you've withdrawn from?

4. When was the last time you blew up or withdrew in anger?
  A. What set you off?
  B. Knowing what you know now, how would you handle the same situation next time?

5. List any people you feel you should repair relationships with, people whom you were angry with, or who were angry with you.

To get a true picture, you may need to ask the opinions of your family, friends, or peers at work.

Disarming the "Booby Traps" to Success

The naive believes everything:
but a wise man looks well to a matter.

—PROVERBS 14:15

Two of my cousins were courageous Marines who served their country in the Vietnam War. Of all the dangers they faced, the ones they feared the most were booby traps, such as hidden antipersonnel mines covered with foliage. In an instant, these devices could permanently maim or kill an unsuspecting soldier.

Solomon reveals that a similar kind of booby trap in your personal or professional life can have an equally devastating effect. What is the name of that booby trap? Naivete. And it can ambush anyone, regardless of their intelligence, education, financial success, or personal achievements.

Philo T. Farnsworth was a genius. In high school, his understanding of physics, mathematics, and the developing science of electronics was light-years ahead of his teachers'. At the age of fourteen, he envisioned a system of electronic line-by-line scanning of an image and the transmission of that image. He began working full-time on the development of the world's first television at the age of nineteen. Many of the world's foremost scientists and engineers and the world's leading manufacturers had determined that the problems of electronically capturing and transmitting visual images were of such a great magnitude that such a device was financially unfeasible. And yet, by the age of twenty-four, Farnsworth was awarded two patents for inventing the television camera and receiver.

Another inventor, Edward H. Armstrong, created a method of sound amplification called frequency modulation (FM), which is the heart of today's quality sound transmission used in radio, television, and cellular telephones. Without Armstrong's FM, there would be no modern sound transmission.

Yet in spite of their indisputable genius and their incalculable contributions to mass communications, neither man substantially profited from his inventions. Nearly bankrupt, Armstrong committed suicide. Farnsworth never received a single penny of the millions of dollars in royalties he had been promised by the electronics company that profited most from his invention.

How could this happen? Solomon answers that question in Proverbs 14:15 when he says, "The naive believe everything, but a wise man looks well into a matter." You see, although these men were geniuses in the world of science, in the world of commerce they were very naive. Farnsworth was so naive that when the CEO of RCA sent a company scientist to see Farnsworth's invention, Farnsworth not only welcomed him, he showed him how to build one of his invention's key components. Farnsworth knew that this scientist had applied for competing patents, yet, according to author Harold Evans, he trusted in "honor among men of science." The scientist Vladimir Zworykin stole his technology and was honored years later as the inventor of television. Armstrong, too, was betrayed by David Sarnoff and RCA, a CEO and a company he had trusted. After years of litigation, near bankruptcy, he jumped out of the thirteenth floor of his apartment building.

⊚⊚ The Cost of Being Naive

In 1993, a friend of mine introduced me to a billionaire who was funding a new company that possessed a revolutionary patented technology. I was so taken with its promise that I invested $2.5 million in his company. In 1998, a friend I had recently made told me he would soon be taking his company public. As a result, I invested $3 million in his company. In 2000, my cousin introduced me to a stock-trading whiz who, in four short years, had turned $5,000 into $14 million. So I invested $2 million with him. Today, these three investments, totaling $7.5 million, have a combined worth of $200,000. That's a 97 percent loss!

What went wrong? I trusted my intuition and took everyone at face value. I had failed to follow Solomon's advice. I violated three of his strongest warnings and as a result crashed and burned. Had I heeded any one of the three, I would be millions of dollars wealthier today. Had I heeded *all* three, today my $7.5 million would, properly invested, be worth nearly $20 million!

∞ Naivete and IQ

Naivete has less to do with intelligence and more to do with the *way* a person approaches individual situations and life in general. A naive person tends to oversimplify a situation and thereby fails to see critical factors that may significantly affect an outcome. As we've seen, geniuses can be just as naive as people of average intelligence. Solomon describes a person as naive when he or she doesn't "look well into a matter" before choosing a course of action. Most people fail to perform due diligence for one or more of the following reasons. Can you identify with any of these?

Oversimplification. We all have a natural inclination toward simplicity. We want things to be simple. We want to be able to figure things out instantly, without having to read an instruction book or doing homework. We want to believe everybody, and we want to accept what we've been told at face value. And sadly, that is foolish. In Proverbs 1:22, Solomon chides, "How long, O naive ones, will you love simplicity?" Important decisions are never simple. There are always important factors hidden beneath the surface that must be searched out and considered.

Presumption. In Proverbs 27:1, Solomon warns, "Do not boast about tomorrow for you do not know what a day may bring forth." Solomon is talking about the attitude and behavior of presumption. We presume that the same conditions and opportunities that are in front of us today will remain available to us in the future—tomorrow, next week, or next year. We naively act on impulse, presuming that we'll have tomorrow to correct any mistakes we make today. We don't look well into a matter before we make the choice, because we can always look into it later. The fact is, however, we do not live in a static world. Everything changes moment by moment, and presuming that we will have the same opportunities or conditions to respond to tomorrow that we have today is both foolish and naive.

Misplaced trust. We often put more trust than we should in people whom we don't know well. More often than not, people are less capable, less experienced, less competent, and less honest than they seem to be. People always put their best foot forward, and we usually make judgments of them in a matter of minutes or seconds. Each of my bad investment decisions was based on taking individuals at face value, believing what they said. None of these three men deserved the level of trust I placed in them. One turned out to be a terribly dishonest person, while the other two were overly optimistic and not qualified to make the kind of forecasts they were making. In each case, I trusted that the individuals were honest and competent in their projections. If I had followed Solomon's admonition and looked well into the matter, digging deeper into their past achievements and representations, I would not have placed my trust in them.

Superficial appearances. Our response to a person or a situation is often based entirely upon appearances. A person may be charismatic or extremely personable, or a business opportunity may appear extraordinary at first glance. But appearances almost never tell enough of the story to base any important decision upon. One of my investment decisions was driven by seeing a prototype of a new product that had been awarded dozens of patents. It appeared to be a technological breakthrough of monumental proportions. What I didn't know was that turning this laboratory prototype into a product that could be economically manufactured would take years longer and cost hundreds of millions of dollars more than the company's executives projected. The company's stock went public at $21 per share in 1998. Today the stock trades at 17 cents per share. So much for appearances!

Laziness. Our natural inclination is to do as little as possible to get what we want. The same is true in the decision-making process. "Looking well into a matter" requires a lot more effort and creativity than simply accepting a statement or person at face value. Our only hope to counter our natural inclination is to apply true diligence to our decision making whenever we are considering an important commitment.

Haste. When we are in a hurry to make a decision, we will usually make it without taking enough time to look into the matter thoroughly. In each of my foolish investment decisions, I was told by the individuals involved that I must act immediately or I was going to miss out on the extraordinary opportunity at hand. In Proverbs 21:5, Solomon warns, "But everyone who is hasty comes *surely* to poverty." Haste is one of the most frequent forms of naivete. How many bad marriages began with one of the individuals pressuring the other one to get married more quickly than she or he wanted? When people push you to hurry, a red flag should go up. Put on the brakes; DON'T let anyone push you to make an important decision in haste. Insist on taking the time to dig deep, seek counsel, and perform the level of diligence necessary to make a wise decision.

Narrow vision. More often than not, our vision is far too limited to make the best decision based only on our own knowledge and experience. Solomon cautions in Proverbs 15:22, "Without counsel plans are frustrated, but with many counselors they succeed." To make important decisions without the aid of outside counsel is not only naive, it's foolish. By bringing in the expert opinion and counsel of others, we radically expand our field of vision and become far more qualified to make a wise decision.

Integrity. Unfortunately, I am convinced that the more honest a person is, the greater his or her inclination to be naive. Why? Honest people never think of lying, stealing, or defrauding someone of their life savings. Such thoughts are so foreign to their character they can't imagine anyone else doing such things to them. Pat Boone and I have been friends for nearly three decades. We used to kid each other about which one of us was more naive. Neither one of us would ever think of swindling people out of their hard-earned savings, so we couldn't imagine anyone doing it to us. And yet it's happened to both of us too many times. My father-in-law is one of the most honest men I have ever known. As one of IBM's most successful salesmen, he was personally recruited by the owners of a smaller computer company. They told him that they would pay him much higher commissions than he was receiving from IBM. He had no reason to doubt their word, because he himself would never make a promise that he wouldn't keep. Besides, these men were active members of his church. So he left a twenty-year career with IBM without looking well into the matter. He delivered a tremendous amount of business to his new employer, but they never paid him the commissions they had promised. He was shocked. How could the owners lie so boldly? His honesty had made him too trusting of men he knew little about and kept him from feeling the need to check out their backgrounds.

Greed. Sometimes we're so anxious to acquire something that we want to believe whatever we are told, hoping this opportunity could be our winning lottery ticket. In each of my investments, I wanted to believe the projections of the optimistic individuals and to ignore all of the warnings from the skeptics on the sidelines. Each was a chance to multiply my money many times over. My focus was blinded by greed, another reason I didn't look well into the matter.

Arrogance. One of the greatest sources of naivete is arrogance. Arrogant people often think they're smarter than everyone else. They don't feel they need to seek outside counsel or perform due diligence—they already know what they need to know. Solomon said, "Pride goes before destruction, and an arrogant spirit before a fall." Sooner or later, arrogant people are blindsided by their arrogance.

Wrong priorities. Sometimes a person chooses not to look in depth into a matter before making an important decision, because they don't think due diligence is that important. They would rather spend their time watching TV, surfing the Internet, playing golf, or doing hundreds of other things of less consequence. Because they don't realize the potential cost of their naivete, they never make overcoming it a priority.

◎ The Solution

Solomon's solution to naivete is one of the most simplistic prescriptions in his writings. He challenges us to "look well into the matter" before we make any important decision. In Chapter 2, we looked at the attribute of diligence—"looking well into a matter," bringing all of the elements of diligence into your decision-making process. Diligence is like a giant floodlight: turn it on, and naivete's darkness disappears.

Some people fear that they will insult others by performing due diligence. They fear a person might ask, "Don't you trust me?" If that happens, your response should be "You haven't given me any reason *not* to trust you, so I do trust everything I know about you. But I never want to make a foolish mistake, and to avoid such mistakes I always follow a simple rule: Look well into a matter before I make any important decision. So that's what I do, no matter who I'm dealing with." If a person is truly honest, they will respect your thoroughness and welcome any due-diligence efforts you undertake.

◎◎ Don't Be Naive When It Comes to Making Wrong Choices

In Proverbs 22:3, Solomon warns us, "The prudent sees the evil and hides himself, But the naive go on, and are punished for it." Most people rarely find themselves in unethical or illegal situations by surprise. Usually, they see a red or yellow flag or two first. At that point, they have a choice. Solomon tells us that a wise man will turn away. Those who are naive, however, see the red flag, feel a twinge in their conscience, and then choose to keep moving in the same direction. This was likely the case with executives at Enron, WorldCom, Tyco, Anderson, and Health South. They saw the red flags and each one of them made a choice. If there were any wise men among them, they would have turned around and looked for another job. Unfortunately, most made the opposite choice. As a result, they lost their jobs and reputations, and some may ultimately lose their freedom. And these were regarded as among the most intelligent and successful people in the corporate world.

They're not alone. How many women and men see red flags go up in new relationships when they are asked to do things that violate their conscience—drugs, alcohol, infidelity? They see the flags, feel the twinge of conscience, and then have to make a choice: "Do I turn around, or do I keep on going?" I've been told by marriage counselors that most victims of domestic violence experienced one or more instances of physical abuse from their mate *before* they got married. They saw the red flag but naively kept with the relationship all the way to the altar. Twenty thousand lives are lost each year from accidents caused by drunk drivers who chose to continue drinking even though they knew they shouldn't. When they stepped into their car, they knew they shouldn't be driving; yet they made a choice and kept on going.

There Is a Way That Seems Right . . .

Solomon warns that we can choose to go down paths that seem right but turn out to be wrong. The cause? We have failed to bring diligence into our decision making. In Proverbs 14:12, he says, "There is a way that seems right to a man, but in the end it leads to death." Diligently looking into a matter will ensure that doesn't happen.

In Proverbs 14:18, Solomon tells us, "The simple inherit folly, but the prudent are crowned with knowledge." In other words, only those who look well into matters before they make important choices will be rewarded. Instead of gaining a reputation as a fool, they'll be rewarded with a reputation as one who is wise.

How to make wise choices.

Don't Deny Your Naivete. Choose to Look Well into Matters. Accept that your natural inclination in decision making will always be to take the path of the lazy or naive. Make the choice to proactively look well into matters before you make important decisions.

Seek Outside Counsel. Over and over again in Proverbs, Solomon cautions us to seek outside counsel. In Proverbs 11:14, he says, "Where no counsel is, the people fall. But in a multitude of counselors, there is safety"; in Proverbs 15:22, he says, "Without counsel plans are frustrated. But with many counselors, they succeed." Later he writes, "Every purpose is established by counsel." His advice is clear, his wisdom undeniable. Follow it.

Without the counsel of my business partners, I never would have succeeded in business. Without the counsel of Dr. Gary Smalley, I would not have the wonderful marriage that I now enjoy. And without the counsel of Solomon, I could not hope for lasting success or happiness.

Choose Your Friends and Associates Wisely. In Proverbs 13:20, Solomon writes, "He that walks with wise men shall become wise. But a companion of fools shall be destroyed." Whom you choose to associate with or partner with can make you or break you. You can be a friend to anyone. But you should be careful about whom you partner with or attach yourself to in any significant way. Look at a person's wisdom and integrity. Be sensitive to any red flags that would warn you of dishonesty. Look at what their priorities are and how they order their lives. How do they treat their parents, spouse, siblings, or children? What do they value most? Don't let yourself become the companion of fools.

Being Prudent Is a Choice You Must Make Every Day

Being prudent is a decision that needs to be made every time you face an important decision in any area of your life. Whether you are facing a business decision, a financial decision, or a personal decision, choose first to "look well into the matter." If you make that choice, and apply the steps we've discussed, you will make wise decisions that will bring you tremendous rewards. If you do not, your natural tendency will lead you down the path of the naive, a path that leads to disappointment and failure.

Knowledge to Wisdom

1. List two or more decisions that you consider to have been major mistakes (personal, business, or financial). For example: a major purchase, a bad investment, taking the wrong job or quitting the right one, a failure in marriage or parenting.

2. Which of the following causes of naivete were contributing factors in those decisions?

___ Oversimplification

___ Presumption

___ Misplaced trust

___ Laziness

___ Superficial appearances

___ Haste

___ Narrow vision

___ Integrity

___ Greed

___ Arrogance

___ Wrong priorities

3. What could you have done differently in your decision-making process that would have enabled you to "look well into the matter" and make a better decision?

4. Einstein defined insanity as doing the same thing over and over again and expecting different results. What can you do differently in your future decision making that will ensure choices that reflect wisdom rather than naivete?

5. List any important decisions that you are currently facing or expect to be facing in the near future.

6. For each of those decisions, write a paragraph about what you will do in your decision-making process to ensure that you will make the best decision possible.

CHAPTER 13
— ❦ —

The Single Biggest Cause
of Financial Loss

So are the ways of every one that is greedy of gain;
which takes away the life of the owners thereof.

—PROVERBS 1:19

Pop Quiz

TRUE OR FALSE:

___ Rich people are greedier than poor and middle-income
people.

___ The more money a person makes, the more greedy they are
likely to be.

___ Greed is not an issue in my life.

When we think of greed, we always think about it in relation
to other people, rather than ourselves. We picture the character Scrooge in Dickens's *A Christmas Carol*. The fact is, the
seeds of greed are present in every human heart. In some
people, these seeds subtly take root and gradually influence
more and more of our decisions, preventing us from achieving what we value most. In others, they grow into giant weeds

that choke the joy out of their lives. The good news is that Solomon shows us how we can prevent greed from taking root and influencing or controlling our lives.

First, let's get a clearer picture of how Solomon defines greed. Did you answer True to any of the questions in the pop quiz above? By Solomon's definition, the right answer to all of the questions in the quiz is False.

◎◎ What Do You Want, and How Badly Do You Want It?

Greed is not just about money. Although greed can certainly drive one's pursuit of riches and material possessions, greed is an attitude that can drive any number of behaviors. Solomon used two Hebrew words to describe greed. One means "to deeply yearn or long for something"; the other implies wanting something so badly that you are willing to violate the rights of others to get it. Combining these two words gives us a fuller picture of what Solomon means. Greed is a deep longing for something that creates a willingness to do whatever it takes to acquire it. In other words, greed is not defined by *what* you want, but rather by *how badly* you want it.

A person can be greedy in just about any imaginable area: the pursuit of power or recognition, the pursuit of love, the pursuit of sexual fulfillment, the pursuit of leisure or a hobby. But in our society, the most visible form of greed is the pursuit of wealth.

GREED is a deep longing for something that drives
us to the point that we are willing to do whatever it
takes to acquire it.

⊚⊚ Greed Can Grow Like a Cancer

Michael Landon was one of my dearest friends in Holly-
wood. He was kind and generous to me in ways that are rarely
seen in the entertainment industry. I had the honor of filming
Mike's last project. A week before our shoot, he took me into
his new home gym. When I asked how he was feeling, he
replied, "Steve, I've never felt better. I'm in the best shape of
my life." Four weeks later, he was rushed to an emergency
room with severe abdominal pain. A few days later, he was
diagnosed with terminal pancreatic and liver cancer. Unlike
more aggressive cancers, pancreatic cancer grows slowly for
years before it produces any noticeable symptoms. In fact, it
usually becomes symptomatic only in its final stage. Mike
died within three months of his diagnosis. My father, on the
other hand, was diagnosed with a very aggressive type of lung
cancer. Dad's cancer was symptomatic within a few months
of its onset. He died seven months after it was diagnosed.

Greed can grow like either one of these cancers—aggressive and obvious from the start, or more subtly and unnoticed until it's inflicted a terrible loss. That is how greed crept
into my life. I was persuaded to make three bad investment
decisions due to my naivete. However, the reason I was susceptible to the optimistic pitches of those who took my

money was that I was greedy—I wanted to make a lot of money quickly. By the time I recognized my greed, it was too late; my life savings had vanished.

๏ Do You Give In to Greed?

If I were to ask you if you have a problem with greed, you would probably answer no and pass a lie-detector test. Yet greed may be subtly taking root in your heart. The fact that it hasn't yet produced an alarming symptom or a devastating consequence does not mean that it is absent or benign. If you don't take preventative or corrective measures, sooner or later it may ultimately rob you of what you value most.

๏ The Consequences of Greed

1. *It can steal your life away.* When I first saw Solomon's warning in Proverbs 1:19, that greed could take away the life of the person who possesses it, I thought it was talking about life only figuratively. After all, I have known countless men and women whose lives were best characterized by greed, and in nearly every case, their lives were also characterized by things like emptiness, lack of purpose, unhappiness, turmoil, and conflict. I now realize that greed can take one's life literally as well. One of my former partners left our company and made millions of dollars in a number of business pursuits. He had a beautiful wife and wonderful children, but his greed robbed him of all of his joy and fulfillment. When his business collapsed and bankruptcy threatened, he went into his garage and took his life.

2. *It can destroy your financial security*. In Proverbs 28:22, Solomon tells us that the person who tries to hurriedly get rich will instead end up in poverty. "He that hastens to be rich has an evil eye, and considers not that poverty shall come upon him." For those focused on getting rich, Solomon says, riches will "sprout wings and fly off like an eagle."

3. *It can affect your loved ones.* If you're like me, I'm sure there are plenty of times when you have thought to yourself, "What I'm doing is *my* business. It has nothing to do with my parents, my wife, or my kids." But in Proverbs 15:27, Solomon warns, "He that is greedy of gain brings trouble into his own house." There is no such thing as your "own" business. What you do affects everyone you care about. And it doesn't matter if that greed for gain is financial, material, or for an appetite or an addiction. In business, we may start out with good intentions. We simply want to make more money so we can provide a better life for our families. But, as the seeds of greed take root, we begin to pursue our careers with such intensity that we neglect the very family we wanted to provide with that better life.

4. *It can bankrupt you spiritually.* In Proverbs 13:7, Solomon writes, "There is he that makes himself rich, yet has nothing." Anyone who has read Howard Hughes's biography has a clear picture of this truth. He was driven by his greed for wealth, power, fame, and love. He was proclaimed the richest man in the world, and yet he had nothing: no lasting happiness, no fulfillment, not even security. You, too, may acquire whatever you are greedy for; but Solomon promises that even when you acquire it, you will have nothing of value.

5. *It can steal your happiness and reason for living*. At first, you just want a little bit more. Then you want a little bit *more*. At first you're thinking about it once in a while. Then you're thinking about it every day, but just a little bit each day. Soon it dominates your focus all day long. You can't be happy or fulfilled because your focus is on what you don't have. You lose what used to be your purpose for living because your life is now centered on chasing what you still lack. That's the nature of greed.

6. *It can steal your integrity*. In Proverbs 28:20, Solomon states, "But he that makes haste to be rich shall not be innocent." Greed is never patient. It's always in a hurry to get that which it covets. It creates the attitude "I want as much as I can get and I want it now!" It fuels your natural drive for instant gratification. In their quest to accelerate their wealth, people become willing to do that which is unethical, immoral, or illegal to acquire more. There's nothing inherently wrong in desiring more. But when that desire becomes our focus, or causes us to set aside our priorities, values, or ethics, it has become greed.

7. *It creates a false sense of security*. In Proverbs 11:28, Solomon writes, "He that trusts in his riches shall fall." Unfortunately, the more money one makes, the more likely he is to become arrogant. He begins to think he can get away with more and more. He takes more risks. And when he falls, he falls hard.

◎◎ Detecting Greed in Its Early Stages

Remember, greed isn't defined by what you *want* but rather by the lengths you will go to get it. Nor is greed just the desire for money or material things. Greed can take control of any desire in our lives: achievement, love, sex, alcohol, wealth, or material possessions. Greed transforms our natural desires into a consuming drive for more, regardless of our best interests or the best interests of others. To keep it from gaining a controlling foothold in our lives, we need to look for the symptoms that will alert us to its presence.

Early warning symptoms of greed

Coveting. All of us see things that others have and feel a momentary desire to have them, too. That's perfectly natural. *Coveting,* on the other hand, is a strong and persistent desire or craving for something that you don't have. It becomes a focus of your thoughts and desires. Acquiring it ultimately becomes a priority in your life, deferring or replacing more important priorities.

More, more, more. As you achieve your goals and acquire the things you want, instead of being grateful for what you have, your focus keeps shifting to what you *don't* have. You find that you have lots of desires but little lasting contentment or joy.

Hurry, hurry. Whatever you're chasing after, you can't get it fast enough. Rather than patiently pursuing what you want and working to earn it, you find yourself looking for short-cuts to obtain it faster. Today, people take on extraordinary credit-card debt because they want so much before they can legitimately afford it.

Closing your eyes to compromise. When you find yourself contemplating compromising your values or integrity to achieve what you want more quickly than would otherwise be likely, you know that greed is overtaking you. By the time you are actually compromising your values, it is too late. The good news is that once you're aware of your tendency toward greed, you can hit the brakes and reverse course.

More turbulence. If you find yourself experiencing more conflict, more adversity, and more problems in general in your life, think about your focus. When our focus continually shifts to what we *don't* have, we create turbulence in our lives and the lives of those around us. That turbulence can be a signal that greed is overtaking our lives.

How Greed Gains a Foothold in Our Hearts

When I graduated from college, I had no financial goals and almost no drive for material things. I simply wanted to succeed in my career and be able to provide the modest material needs of my family. By the time my second child was born, I was deep in debt and barely making enough money to pay our bills. After many failures, I started a new business with my partners. It was an exciting time. Before I knew it, my focus had shifted from my family life to making our business successful. I was traveling 160 days a year, working on project after project. Then 160 days turned into 230 days. By our tenth year in business, I was spending nearly 300 days a year on the road. I wasn't working so hard for the money or for material possessions. My greed was for creating more and more successful projects. I loved my work. But in the process, I sacrificed my family. I could have sworn I wasn't greedy, because money wasn't my focus. But the truth is, I *was* greedy—for achievement and the praise and appreciation of my partners.

Greed can infect any goal. It can even distort your relationships with your spouse or your children—through possessiveness (wanting more time and attention than another person is able to give you).

Can I Achieve Extraordinary Success Without Being Greedy?

You may be thinking, "Now, wait a minute. The reason I bought this book was to learn Solomon's secrets for achieving greater success and wealth." Well, you *can* achieve extraordinary success and increase your wealth by using Solomon's secrets. There's nothing wrong or immoral about wanting to achieve success. It becomes immoral only when that desire is colored by greed. True success is a natural by-product of Solomon's wisdom on diligence, communication, partnering, and the other subjects I've covered in this book. The key is keeping your efforts to succeed in the right perspective. Be on the alert for warning symptoms of greed; seek the counsel of others who care about you and your family. Doing so will enable you to keep greed from gaining a foothold in your heart and in your life.

◎ Solomon's Guidelines for Achieving Success Without Greed

Solomon offers several guidelines for acquiring success and wealth.

Focus on achievement rather than money. What do you *really* want to achieve with your life, your family, your career, or a particular job or project? When you know what you want to achieve, then it's simply a matter of applying what you've learned about diligence and the other strategies we've discussed. In Proverbs 14:23, Solomon wrote, "In all labor there is profit. But mere talk leads only to poverty." If you apply true diligence to your labor in any project, you *will* experience significant success most of the time—as long as your drive for achievement doesn't cause you to set aside any of your more important values or priorities.

Use your labor to achieve financial success, rather than chasing wealth in other pursuits. Solomon says in all labor there is profit. He tells us to bring diligence and excellence into our labor. My labor is marketing. Warren Buffett's labor is investing. I have made a lot of money through my work and lost a lot of money by trying to make money in fields outside of my field of expertise. If you bring diligence and excellence into your labors, you will make money. If you apply Solomon's wisdom to spending (limiting your debt to appreciating assets), then your savings will grow. If you apply his wisdom to investing (seeking a multitude of counselors and not trying to get rich quick), then your investments will grow at a significant rate.

Don't try to *get rich*. Solomon clearly teaches us *not* to set our focus on getting rich. Doing so is the quickest way to go broke. In Proverbs 23:4–5, he writes, "Do not wear yourself out to get rich; have the wisdom to show restraint. Cast but a glance at riches, and they are gone, for they will surely sprout wings and fly off to the sky like an eagle." The times I've invested in projects with the intent of getting rich, I've lost my investment. On the other hand, when I have kept my focus on achieving goals through my labor, I've had more success than I could have ever imagined. Everyone wants to win a lottery. Everyone wants to get rich with as little effort as possible. But for every one out of 50 million people who hold a winning lottery ticket, there are 49,999,999 who throw their tickets (and money) in the trash. The same is true with get-rich-quick schemes. For every winner, there are millions of losers. On the other hand, 100 out of every 100 people who apply diligence and excellence to their labor will ultimately succeed. Although it involves a lot more effort, I like those odds a whole lot better.

Acquire success and wealth the *right* way, which brings no sorrow. As you work to acquire success and wealth, how can you tell if greed is your driving force? Solomon answers that question in Proverbs 10:22 where he writes, "It is the blessing of the LORD that makes rich, and He adds no sorrow to it." If your pursuit of success has caused you to lose your spouse, your children, your values, your ethics, or your integrity, then greed has probably been a driving force. On the other hand, if you achieve success without discarding your values or neglecting your family, then God is free to bless you; and you can escape the sorrows that often accompany success and wealth in today's culture.

How to overcome greed.

How can we remove greed once we've been affected by it?

Develop a trust-based relationship with God. In Proverbs 3:5-6 Solomon writes, "Trust in the LORD with all your heart and do not lean on your own understanding. In all your ways acknowledge Him, and He will make your paths straight." Notice he doesn't say trust in a religion or a church. His focus is on God and a trust-based relationship with Him. Solomon tells us that if we acknowledge God in everything we do— *before* we do it and *as* we do it—then he promises that God himself will direct our paths. God will never direct a person in a path of greed, because greed is an attribute that is contrary to God's loving and generous nature. It is impossible to acknowledge God in all your ways and walk down a highway of greed at the same time.

Set your focus on giving generously to others in need. In Proverbs 21:26, Solomon says, "The righteous gives and spares not." Generosity is both the vaccine and the antidote to greed. The fastest way to eliminate greed from your life is to make a concentrated effort to give to others. You don't have to wait until you're rich to become generous. You can be generous with your time, your kindness, your words of encouragement, your labor, and whatever money or material possessions you have. Rick Warren, the author of *The Purpose-*

Driven Life, when asked what he was doing with the millions of dollars in royalties he was receiving from the sales of his book, said the first thing he did was to pay back the twenty years of wages his church had paid him. He and his wife were "reverse tithers," meaning they were keeping 10 percent for themselves and giving 90 percent of the royalties to a charity they established to meet the needs of others throughout the world. But his giving began long before his megasuccessful book. His next statement was what impressed me the most. He said that when he first became the pastor of his church, he and his wife agreed that they would give 10 percent of their income to the needs of others, and that every year they would increase their charitable giving by an extra percentage point. After ten years, they were giving 20 percent of their income to charity, and after twenty years they were giving 30 percent. And that was on a church pastor's salary, *before* his book took off.

Stop chasing riches. In Proverbs 23:7, Solomon tells us, "As a man thinks in his heart, so is he." If your thoughts and emotions are focused on getting rich, then you *will* become infected by greed. Instead, let your thoughts focus on achievement and on generously meeting the genuine needs of others.

Don't Be Fooled by the Nature of Greed

A friend of mine once told me a tragic story from his childhood. His mother took him to a traveling circus that had come to town. He recalled how a snake trainer stepped into a cage with a giant python. As he had done many times before, the trainer stood motionless as the python began to wrap himself around his body. Then, to everybody's horror, the snake began to constrict. The trainer's facial expression told the crowd that something was terribly wrong. He couldn't scream, because the air was being squeezed out of his lungs. Then the crowd heard his bones beginning to crack. By the time other trainers had moved into the cage, the trainer was dead. My friend asked me, "Do you know what mistake the snake trainer made?" When I shook my head no, he said, "He thought he had tamed the snake. But you cannot change the snake's nature."

The same is true with greed. We think that we can control a little greed in our lives, but we can't. We can't take the greed out of greed. Let it gain a little foothold in our life, and it will *ultimately* steal your life—either figuratively or literally.

Knowledge to Wisdom

DETECTING THE SEEDS OF GREED IN YOUR LIFE

1. Look for any of the following warning symptoms of greed in your life.

___ Do you covet what other people have?

___ No matter what you get, do you soon want more?

___ Do you find yourself in a hurry to get what you want?

___ Do you compromise your priorities, values, or ethics to get what you want?

___ Are you experiencing less contentment and fulfillment?

___ Are you experiencing more turbulence in your pursuits or in life in general?

2. Do you have a problem with greed in:

___ Your job or career?

___ Your investment or savings efforts?

___ Your desire to acquire things?

___ Your relationships?

___ Your leisure activities or hobbies?

3. Describe the specific actions you can take to turn away from greed.

4. Do you use credit cards to purchase non-necessities before you can afford them?

5. What should you do to stop buying non-necessities before you can truly afford them?

—☙☙—

CHAPTER 14

Defeating the Enemy of Happiness and Success

> Pride goes before destruction,
> and an arrogant spirit before a fall.
>
> —PROVERBS 16:18

☙☙ The Attitude That Precedes a Fall

The one attitude that can cause the most devastating consequences in both your personal and business life is pride, also referred to as arrogance or conceit. It is an attitude whose seeds are present within all of us. It has destroyed the lives of individuals, unraveled families, undermined corporations, and even caused the fall of entire nations. It can creep into one's spirit almost unnoticed, or it can come upon a person suddenly, like a tsunami upon a quiet coastal village. It is an attitude that all of us must deal with throughout our lives. We confront it every day in one way or another. When recognized and dealt with, it can be kept in check, its destructive power neutralized. When ignored or nurtured, it can grow like a cancer.

One of the most anticipated and highly viewed events of the Winter Olympics is the women's figure skating finals. In

2002, Michelle Kwan was the reigning World Champion and the odds-on favorite for winning. The morning before the event, Katie Couric conducted an interview with Michelle on *The Today Show,* asking her why she had ended her relationship with her longtime coach prior to the Olympic Games. Michelle told Katie that she wanted the world to know she could win on her own, without the help of a coach. Katie pointed out that Michelle was going to have her father in the place where her coach would have been. Michelle answered, "Yes, but *not* as a coach. He's just going to be there for emotional support."

At that moment, I turned to my wife and said, "She's not going to win!" "Why do you say that?" Shannon replied. "Because pride has become the basis of her decision . . . she's going to have a fall." Michelle wanted the world to know that she and she alone would be the reason for her win, not her coach's strategy or coaching skills. Sadly, as I predicted, that night, in the midst of one of the most important events of her life, Michelle fell. And the crown jewel of her career, an Olympic Gold Medal, was lost.

The same night, I watched a sixteen-year-old U.S. skater named Sarah Hughes prepare to take her turn on the ice. I noticed she and her coach engaged in last-minute conversation. I saw how intently she looked into her coach's eyes, taking in every word. She nodded, smiled brightly, and skated into the arena. "Watch this," I told my wife. "She's going to give the performance of her life." Shannon asked, "How do you know?" "Look how humble she is. She's soaking up her coach's advice like a sponge. She doesn't think she has a chance of winning, so the pressure's off. She's just going to go out there, have a good time doing what she loves most, and try to perform like never before." And that's exactly what she did. In fact, she performed a move—a quadruple jump—so difficult that no woman skater had attempted it before in a competition. She pulled it off flawlessly—not just once, but twice. And the Gold was hers.

I tell this story not as a criticism of Michelle Kwan. She is a World Champion many times over and one of the world's all-time great figure skaters. I share it because to me, Michelle's actions provided a vivid picture of pride and its consequences, while Sarah's behavior showed the rewards of humility. All of us struggle with pride. I have lost millions of dollars and experienced agonizing personal and business failures because pride and arrogance colored my thinking.

Pride is often subtle; we don't even know we're being influenced by it. It was pride that was behind Solomon's downfall. In spite of unlimited power, wealth, and wisdom, he lost nearly everything he valued because of pride. Solomon knew that pride could bring about his downfall. He wrote, "Pride goes before destruction and an arrogant spirit before a fall." Yet pride is such a cunning and implacable enemy that even when you know its destructive power, you can succumb to its seductive call.

Fast-forward nearly 2,800 years. The statement most often used by insiders and vendors to describe the executives of Enron was "extreme arrogance." That arrogance cost the life of one executive, the destruction of the reputations of others, the jobs and life savings of thousands of employees, and the loss of tens of billions of dollars by their investors, creditors, and suppliers. Treating pride as a common and relatively harmless social gaffe is as foolish as mistaking a deadly ebola virus for the common cold.

◎◎ You Can't Beat an Enemy You Don't Understand

What does Solomon mean by the words "arrogance" and "pride"? He doesn't mean the emotion you feel when your son or daughter scores the winning goal in a soccer match. He's talking about a transformation that takes place in our heart. The Hebrew word is derived from a word that means "swollen" or "high." A proud or arrogant person has a swollen ego. He or she thinks they are better than others, more deserving than others. He tends to believe that he is solely responsible for what he has achieved. He takes credit for the good things in his life and blames others for the bad things.

Pride is not limited to any economic or social class. It's found among the rich and the poor, the educated and the uneducated. Its root cause is self-centeredness. We want to be the ultimate authority of our life. Deep down we want everyone else to meet all of our needs, desires, and expectations. We act as if our needs, desires, and expectations are more important than those of others. Ask a hundred people, "Do you succumb to pride or arrogance in your life?" and at least ninety-nine will answer no. The tragedy is, if you don't think you have a problem with pride, then you will do nothing to overcome its influence in your life.

◉◉ The Consequences of Pride

No hope for lasting happiness. In Proverbs 26:12, Solomon wrote, "Seest thou a man wise in his own conceit? There is more hope for a fool." In other words, a person whose conceit makes him think that he is better or smarter than he is has less hope of gaining anything of true worth in life than a fool.

When I set aside the advice of my counselors and the people who cared about me to make those bad investment decisions, what spurred me on was my greed. But underneath that was arrogance. I set their counsel aside because I thought I knew better than everybody else. *That* is pride, through and through.

Conflict. If you are in a relationship in which arguments seem to break out over nothing, it should be a tip-off that either you or the other person has a problem with pride. According to Solomon, a proud person doesn't just attract contention, he or she *causes* it. "He that is of a proud heart stirs up strife." Solomon went so far as to say that pride is the primary source of contention. The person ruled by pride is validated only when others agree with his or her point of view. He sees disagreement as a personal affront to his esteem. As a consequence, any disagreement must be attacked. If you find yourself being argumentative, then it's time to consider the part pride plays in your attitude and behavior.

A downfall. In Proverbs 18:12, Solomon warns, "Before his downfall a man's heart is proud." When I was seventeen, the Air Force sent me and eleven other Civil Air Patrol cadets to a program in which we would learn to fly a sailplane (glider). In the early days of the course, the four instructor pilots placed bets on which one of them would have the first student to fly solo. In his haste to win the bet, my instructor, early in my training, jumped out of my glider, slammed down the canopy, and signaled the tow plane to take me into the air for my first solo flight. Knowing that I was not ready, I was extremely humble in my approach to that flight, executing each stage of the flight with extreme care. My flight was a great success, and my instructor won the wager. Later that day, after most of the other students had soloed, there was time for one more flight. I was quick to jump into the glider, thinking I was now ready for anything. Pride swelled my head and blurred my vision. Initially, the flight went well—I was able to navigate the thermals (rising columns of air) for nearly forty-five minutes on a flight that should have lasted only fifteen. Unfortunately, in my arrogance, I flew too far away from the airfield and became lost and disoriented. Because gliders have no engine, you go down when the thermals disappear, and there's nothing you can do about it. I ended up landing more than a mile away from the field and was humiliated by my instructor in front of the entire corps of cadets. It was just one of many downfalls in my life that followed when pride governed my thinking.

In my business, I have produced a number of marketing campaigns that we refer to in the industry as "grand-slam home runs"—projects that have produced hundreds of millions of dollars in sales. Sometimes those projects have been followed by projects that were giant losers. Why? Because my home runs often resulted in arrogance, which led to the failures that followed.

Disgrace and humiliation. In Proverbs 11:2, Solomon writes that when pride rears its head, "then comes disgrace." "A man's pride will bring him low," he claims. Can you imagine the disgrace and depression that come when you lose your life savings because you went against the advice of everyone you admire and love? Can you imagine your feelings when you've pushed your partners to go forward with a project to which they commit thousands of hours and invest millions of dollars, only to see it fail? These are a few of the things I have experienced as a result of my arrogance. I could give you many others. Humility or humiliation. Solomon gives us a simple choice. In any given situation, we can let humility, or pride, guide our decisions and behavior. When we allow our pride to rule, painful humiliation usually follows.

Separation from God. If you are a true atheist, you won't worry about this consequence. But for believers and agnostics, this is without a doubt the most serious consequence of pride. In Proverbs 15:25 Solomon warns, "The LORD will tear down the house of the proud." And in Proverbs 16:5 he writes, "Everyone who is proud in heart is an abomination to the Lord. Assuredly, he will not be unpunished." How would you like God to consider you an abomination and promise to punish you and destroy your heritage? That's what Solomon says will be the ultimate destiny of the proud and arrogant. You may object, pointing out proud and arrogant people who are rich and seem to have everything life could offer. But Solomon doesn't say that God's punishment will necessarily be administered quickly or even in the person's lifetime. If God exists and is truly eternal, as Solomon believed, then He has all eternity to exact His punishment. Because of Solomon's pride and the resulting choices he made, he lost everything he valued during his life, but his kingdom and heritage were not destroyed until *after* his death. All things considered, I'd much rather have God as my friend and ally.

◎◎ Effectively Dealing with Pride

It is critical that we learn how to detect pride's presence and effectively deal with it. In the early 1970s, I worked for a large bank that was visited by a U.S. Treasury agent who was an expert on counterfeit money. When asked how long he had been studying counterfeit bills, he answered, "I don't study counterfeit bills, I only study real ones." He explained that by gaining a thorough knowledge of every square centimeter of a genuine twenty-, fifty-, and hundred-dollar bill, he could nearly always spot a phony bill instantly. The same is true with pride. The best way to recognize it is to understand the nature of true humility. By becoming thoroughly familiar with its characteristics, we can quickly identify its absence. And when humility is absent, pride is usually in control.

What *is* true humility? It's not a person covering themselves in sackcloth and ashes and exclaiming, "Woe is me." True humility begins with a heartfelt belief that others have made it possible for you to have everything in life that you value. When a person truly believes that, they carry with them the eager and grateful spirit of a learner, one who welcomes and values the input and contributions of others. It is easy for a learner to honor the opinions, points of view, and the genuine needs of others. In fact, one of the most admired traits of the truly humble is their inclination, when necessary, to put other people's needs above their own.

My former church pastor, Dr. Jim Borror, while visiting a church in the Northwest, was asked by a woman to meet with her husband, a multimillionaire entrepreneur with thousands of employees. Although this man had tens of millions of dollars and everything money could buy, he was unhappy, bitter, and cantankerous. No one liked being around him, and contention and strife followed him wherever he went. He was disliked by his employees and even his children. His wife barely tolerated him.

When he met the man, Dr. Borror listened to him talk about his accomplishments and quickly realized that pride ruled this man's heart and mind. He claimed he had single-handedly built his company from scratch. Even his parents hadn't given him a dime. He had worked his way through college.

Jim said, "So you did everything by yourself."

"Yep," the man replied.

Jim repeated, "No one ever gave you anything."

"Nothing!"

So Jim asked, "Who changed your diapers? Who fed you as a baby? Who taught you how to read and write? Who gave you jobs that enabled you to work your way through college? Who gave you your first job after college? Who serves food in your company's cafeteria? Who cleans the toilets in your company's rest rooms?" The man hung his head in shame. Moments later, with tears in his eyes, he said, "Now that I think about it, I haven't accomplished anything by myself. Without the kindness and efforts of others, I probably wouldn't have anything." Jim nodded and asked, "Don't you think they deserve a little thanks?"

That man's heart was transformed, seemingly overnight. In the months that followed, he wrote thank-you letters to every person he could think of who had made a contribution to his life. He wrote individual thank-you notes to every one of his 3,000 employees. He not only felt a deep sense of gratitude, he began to treat everyone around him with respect and appreciation. When Dr. Borror visited him a year or two later, he could hardly recognize him. Happiness and peace had replaced the anger and contention in his heart. He looked years younger. His employees loved him for treating them with the honor and respect that true humility engenders.

◉◉ The Rewards That Money Can't Buy

Honor and support. While pride will bring a man or woman down, humility will raise him or her up. Solomon says, "But, honor shall uphold the humble in spirit." When Solomon talks about humility, he's talking about a humility that permeates who you are; those who are "humble in spirit" view others as important as themselves. He or she also views what they have with gratitude, recognizing the contributions that others have made to their lives. To those who live with humility, Solomon says that honor shall support them through good times and bad.

Minnie Aiton, at the age of sixteen, began attending college as a math major. She had a genius IQ and a photographic memory. But, with the advent of the Great Depression, she quit college to become an administrative assistant to the founder of a tiny savings and loan in Arizona. She was the firm's fifth employee. Eventually, the company grew into one of the largest financial institutions in America. As it grew, Minnie not only performed her prescribed duties, she trained nearly every manager in the organization in a myriad of skills and disciplines. She had a reputation for knowing more about the savings-and-loan business than anyone in the state. She was known as the woman anyone could take their problems to. I was told by the company's CEO that she was without doubt the most admired and beloved person in the company. At her funeral, I was told by one person, "Whenever you were around Minnie, you felt like you were the most important person on earth; you knew she cared and would do anything to help you." Near the end of her career, she was approached by an attorney who told her what she had been told by countless others: "If you were a man, they would have made you a senior vice president years ago." He told her that if she would let him represent her he could win millions of dollars in a lawsuit. Her response? "Why would I ever sue First Federal? For forty years they have provided a paycheck every two weeks, paid for all my vacations and my family's health care." And with that, my dear mother turned down his offer. Her humility was well known to all. She was the favorite aunt of her twenty-seven nieces and nephews, the favorite relative of her cousins, aunts, uncles, and in-laws. Honor followed her throughout her eighty-six years of life.

Wisdom. In Proverbs 11:2, Solomon claims that "with humility comes wisdom." In other words, the more humble you are, the more wise you become. Unlike the proud, who believe they know everything, the humble value what others can teach them. They become like a sponge, soaking up wisdom from every experience and person they encounter.

Peace, harmony, a valued heritage, and friendship with God. In addition to wisdom and honor, a person who is humble enjoys the benefits that are the converse of pride's consequences. Pride creates strife and contention, which means that humility creates peace and harmony. A proud person's heritage will be destroyed, while a humble person's heritage will live on for generations. And if God sets himself against the proud, as He has stated again and again, then He must certainly become an ally to the humble.

◎◎ Replacing Pride with Humility

Humility and pride cannot coexist in the heart at the same moment in time. The presence of one will eliminate the other. In other words, rather than concentrating on uprooting pride from the heart, we do much better to discover what we can do to bring humility into our thinking and interactions.

Be grateful. Begin to focus more often on the good things in your life, on the incredible contributions others have made to that which you value most. Make a list of the things you value, starting with the most important first. The longer your list is, the better. For example, the top items of my list are my relationship with God, my family, their health, my health, my dear friends, the clarity of my mind, my ability to make a living, my partners, and the success of our businesses. Although I acknowledge my contribution to each of these, not one of these would be mine to enjoy without the contributions of others. Next to each item on your own list, write down the names of people who have helped you in that area of your life. As you begin to see all of the contributions others have made to your life, a spirit of gratefulness will naturally begin to emerge. As it does, your humility will grow.

Become more attentive to and focused upon the needs of others. Shift more of your focus to contributing to the needs of others. Your gratefulness and humility will grow. Why was Mother Teresa so humble? It wasn't because of what she had or didn't have, or because of anything we can remember her saying. It was because her entire life was devoted to meeting the needs of other people. She was so focused on meeting their needs that she paid little attention to the material things she lacked in life. But you don't have to live a life of sacrifice on the scale of Mother Teresa. You simply need to become more attentive to the needs of others and more grateful for what you have.

◎◎ Final Thoughts

Let me leave you with three additional insights that Solomon offers on the subject of pride.

Arrogance and laziness. Solomon tells us in Proverbs 26:16 that a sluggard or lazy person is wiser in his own eyes and conceit than seven wise men. In other words, those who are lazy don't work because they think they're better than people who do.

Pride and the rich. In Proverbs 28:11, Solomon tells us that a rich man thinks that because he's rich he's wise, and therefore ceases to hold on to the spirit of a learner. The poor man, on the other hand, realizes his need for more understanding and wisdom, and actively searches for it.

Don't partner with the arrogant. In Proverbs 16:19, Solomon writes, "It is better to be of a humble spirit with the lowly, than to divide the spoil with the proud." In other words, it's better to remain humble and befriend humble people than to associate with an arrogant man.

Solomon knew more about pride than perhaps anyone who has ever lived. And yet, midway through his life, he set aside his knowledge about pride and fell victim to it. The same can happen to any one of us. We need to be constantly vigilant, and on the lookout for symptoms of pride in our lives. In the "Knowledge to Wisdom" section that follows, I suggest a checklist that you can use to take a periodic "pride checkup." Regularly review your list of the contributions others have made to your life; add to it regularly. If pride can bring about the fall of the wisest, richest, and most powerful man on earth, think of the impact it can have on your own life.

Knowledge to Wisdom

1. Create a "gratefulness list," as I discussed earlier. Review it and add to it daily.

2. Use the checklist below. Has humility or pride governed your attitudes and activities?

SYMPTOMS-OF-PRIDE CHECKLIST

DO YOU:

- Ignore or neglect the needs of others?
- View most things from your perspective instead of trying to understand the other person's point of view?
- Speak quickly and listen slowly with colleagues, friends, or family members?
- Concentrate on what you want to say next rather than focus on what the other person is trying to say?
- Measure your success by your job, title, salary, or possessions?

ARE YOU:

- Argumentative?
- Quick to blame others for problems or failures?
- Slow to admit when you are wrong?
- Uninterested in the opinions and feelings of others?
- Quick to look down on others?

— ◎◎ —

CHAPTER 15

Solomon's Foundation for Success

How much better is it to get wisdom than gold!
And to get understanding is to be chosen over silver.

—PROVERBS 16:16

◎◎ The Critical Difference Between Wisdom and Knowledge

In ancient societies, houses were often built without a foundation. However, builders ultimately learned a very hard lesson. Even though such structures offered shelter in good weather, they weren't dependable in the face of storms. In fact, storms often demolished entire communities. Today, no architect would consider designing a building without a foundation. It is the foundation that gives a building the integrity upon which all of the other structural supports must rely. Without a solid foundation, nothing significant can be built to endure.

The same is true in our business and personal lives. Yet most adults build their personal and business lives without a sturdy foundation. They face each day without a well-thought-out plan. They may carry their day planners or PDAs filled with to-do lists that reflect their intentions for the day. But they live their lives from day to day, constantly reacting to every wind of change. When they encounter the unexpected storms of life, they are quickly unsettled, and they often make bad decisions or choices, sometimes with devastating consequences.

You don't need to have a high IQ to become wise!

A friend of mine was the head of an engineering team that designed and built the world's most advanced mainframe computer in 1976. As he was telling me of its many advancements, he proudly proclaimed that it could receive more than one billion bytes of information per second. I asked him how many it could receive and process simultaneously. He looked a little puzzled and then replied, "Well, only one." I asked him what he would think of a computer that could receive and process millions of bytes simultaneously. "That's impossible," he replied. So I told him that the human brain receives and processes over two million bytes of information simultaneously, from *each* eye. Add together all of the other bytes it processes from the other four senses and all of the inputs it receives from the organs and cells throughout the body, and the number rises to tens of millions of bytes simultaneously. While his computer filled an entire room, this computer was miniaturized to fit within a space of a few cubic inches.

My point? Each of us has the world's most advanced computer. It is capable of producing levels of achievement

beyond anything most of us have ever imagined. But to opti-
mize its use and achieve the high levels of success and happiness that each of us is capable of attaining, our computer
must be programmed with the right software. And Solomon
offers the greatest software system ever packaged. He calls it
"wisdom."

Our IQ, or level of raw intelligence, is something each of
us is born with. But you don't have to have a high IQ or be an
academic scholar to acquire wisdom. A good many geniuses
have acted foolishly, and the world's most highly educated
scholars have no better track record in the area of personal
happiness or material success than the rest of us. At the same
time, the vast majority of the world's most successful people
(including Edison, Rockefeller, Henry Ford, Clara Barton,
Helen Keller, and Oprah Winfrey) were neither scholars *nor*
geniuses. But, at critical times in their lives, they made wise
decisions that catapulted their achievements from mediocrity
to the stars.

Acquiring true wisdom provides a solid foundation from
which you can make a lifetime of wise decisions. Solomon
provides specific steps that we can take to become wise individuals. This wisdom is not passive, but rather extremely
active. It can produce a lifetime of extraordinary success and
happiness.

Wisdom is infinitely different from mere knowledge. The
difference between knowledge and wisdom is the difference
between reading about a billionaire and being one. Would you
rather learn about billionaires or become one? Knowledge is

simply the acquiring of information. We live in the information age. We can acquire more information in a day than our grandparents could in a year. But acquiring information does not in itself create success, joy, or lasting fulfillment.

Understanding is learning how to distinguish between information that is true and practical, and information that is not. Understanding places great value on truth and its practical application.

Wisdom goes one step further. It takes those truths that have the greatest value and correctly applies them to situations, circumstances, or to life in general.

KNOWLEDGE: **The acquiring of information.**
UNDERSTANDING: **Discerning and valuing important and practical truths.**
WISDOM: **The act of *applying* valued truths to any given situation and to life in general.**

◉◎ Acquiring Wisdom

Solomon places a great value on acquiring understanding and an even higher value on the application of wisdom. Here are some of the benefits he promises to those who build their lives on a foundation of wisdom:

A Checking Account of Knowledge. Imagine having a bank account so big that anytime you needed anything, you could simply write a check for it, regardless of the amount.

The wise man, Solomon says, stores knowledge in such a "wisdom account." He can draw upon it whenever he encounters any need or any situation that requires a wise decision. Whether he needs a solution in a time of trouble or wisdom to capitalize on an opportunity, he'll always have plenty of knowledge to draw upon. Not so for the foolish. In Proverbs 10:14, Solomon writes, "Wise men store up knowledge, but with the mouth of the foolish, ruin is at hand."

Understanding **Why** *You Act the Way You Do*. How many times have you done something stupid or out of character and thought, "Why on earth did I do that?" or "What was I thinking?" If you don't understand your behavior, you will repeat it again and again. This is not the case when you acquire wisdom. As Solomon says in Proverbs 14:8, "The wisdom of the prudent is to understand his ways." As you begin to more clearly understand your behavior and natural inclinations, you will begin to make the best choices rather than those to which you're naturally inclined.

A Fountain of Life. Most of us remember from our American history classes that Ponce de León was the first European to set foot in Florida. He was searching for the Fountain of Youth. He never found it, because no such fountain exists. Solomon reveals a much more practical and miraculous fountain in Proverbs 16:22. He calls it a "fountain of life." What is it? Understanding. Like a fountain, understanding not only brings life to your deepest needs and desires, it makes you a source of life to those around you as well.

The Favor of Those in Authority. When you were a child,

nothing was better than having a coach or a teacher smile at
you and pat you on the back and say, "Way to go! Great job!"
The same is true for adults. We hate having a person in
authority mad at us, whether it is our spouse, our boss, or a
police officer. Solomon tells us that when we act wisely we
will gain the favor of those in authority (Proverbs 14:35). He
also says, "A man shall be commended according to his wisdom" (Proverbs 12:8). A commendation is praise accompa-
nied by an award. In business, that award is usually a bonus or
pay increase.

   Value and Honor. According to Gary Smalley, the number-one desire of a man is to be admired. And *everyone*—man,
woman, boy, and girl—wants to feel valued. And Solomon
tells us that the one sure way to be valued and honored is to
become wise: "The wise will inherit honor."

   Riches. Solomon is talking about both material and spiritual riches. Material riches can be measured in terms of port-
folios, bank accounts, and possessions. Spiritual riches are
measured by the love, fulfillment, joy, peace, and purpose you
experience and the needs of others that you help fulfill. Too
many people sacrifice spiritual riches in their pursuit of material riches. I'm convinced that attaining material riches
requires much less wisdom than acquiring spiritual ones.
Solomon tells us that wise men and women can acquire both.
"The crown of the wise," he says, "is their riches" (Proverbs
14:24). Notice he says that riches are the crown, rather than
the heart or soul, of the wise. The *heart* of the wise is centered on a value system that reflects true wisdom and the

spiritual values and priorities that wisdom brings. That's why the richest man who ever lived could say with authority, "How much better is it to get wisdom than gold! And to get understanding is to be chosen over getting silver."

Protection and Safety. In Proverbs 2:11–12, Solomon writes, "Discretion will protect you, and understanding will guard you. Wisdom will save you from the ways of wicked men, from men whose words are perverse." Wisdom protects us not only from dangerous situations but, equally important, from falling prey to people driven by unethical values, motives, or intentions: the person who wants to con you out of your life savings, or the business associate who wants you to close your eyes to an unethical decision or practice. He's talking about gaining a level of discernment that can see right through the facades of unscrupulous people of all types. Solomon says that this same discernment, understanding, and wisdom will protect a man or woman from those who would seduce them into compromising situations.

Long Life. Those who build their lives on a foundation of wisdom actually live longer. Accept wisdom, Solomon says, and "the years of your life will be many" (Proverbs 4:10). Once again he distinguishes between knowledge and wisdom. Let me give you another example of the difference. Nearly everyone knows that not wearing seat belts in a car can cost you your life; and yet half of the annual 43,000 fatalities in automobile accidents are people who were not wearing their seat belts. Nearly everyone knows that smoking will shorten your life; yet every year hundreds of thousands of Americans die from diseases caused by smoking. It's not enough to know information. To reap the rewards Solomon promises, you must acquire and consistently exercise wisdom.

◎◎ The Consequences of Not Gaining Wisdom

A Life Without Purpose, Fulfillment, and Happiness. In Proverbs 21:16, Solomon says, "The man that wanders out of the way of understanding shall remain in the congregation of the dead." That's pretty strong talk. He's talking about those people who are physically alive but spiritually dead, those whose lives are not built upon values. Because their hopes, dreams, and values are based upon the temporal, they are ultimately bruised and battered by the winds of change and the storms of life. They may be happy or fulfilled for a season, but when their circumstances change, their happiness and fulfillment slip away. They line up for the therapist's couch and the plastic surgeon's operating table. A life built upon wisdom is never stripped of its purpose, joy, or value. Would you like to simply "get by"? That is the destiny, Solomon says, of the life that is not built upon a foundation of true wisdom.

Decisions That Look Good but End Badly. So many times in life we think we're making the right choice, only to discover that it was the wrong choice. Recently, a woman in my community, driving her little girl to a friend's house, was shot by her ex-husband as he drove up next to her car. Then he turned the gun to his head and killed himself. A few years ago, when the woman was madly in love with this man, she believed that she was making the right choice when she married him. She saw signs of his uncontrollable temper, but she surely never thought he would turn his anger toward her. After all, he was as much in love with her as she was with him. In Proverbs 14:12, Solomon warns, "There is a way that seems right to a man, but in the end it leads to death." Without wisdom there is no way we can have an assurance that the decisions we make will be right not only for the moment but, more important, for life.

Self-deception. "What did I do?" "I wasn't doing anything wrong." "Everybody else was doing the same thing." According to one police officer, these are the three most common things people say when he pulls them over for traffic violations. They *really believe* that they haven't done anything wrong. Solomon said, "Every man's way is right in his own sight." The consequences of self-deception can be ruinous. Self-deception stalks everyone who fails to build a life with a foundation of wisdom. For me, the most extreme example of this was Adolf Hitler's suicide note. At the end of World War II, after exterminating millions of Jews, with his nation's capital little more than piles of rubble and the whole nation in ruins, he opened his suicide note with the words "I die with a happy heart." He goes on to say that he knew his nation one day would unite to continue the work he had begun, and that "international Jewry must bear sole responsibility for the war."

We all experience self-deception in some way, shape, or form in our lives. To avoid self-deception, we need a moral compass. According to Solomon, the only compass that can enable us to clearly see and choose the best paths in life is wisdom. Without that compass, we will make choices that seem fine at the moment but will ultimately lead to disappointment or worse.

Foolish Decisions. Solomon's greatest disdain was reserved for those he categorized as fools. Now, we all make foolish decisions at different times in life, but that does not make us fools. Solomon's definition of a fool is a person whose life is built upon unwise decisions—building on sand rather than a firm foundation. Ty Cobb was arguably the greatest baseball player in history, setting more than ninety major league records during his career. He amassed a fortune as a result of making one good investment. And yet only three people attended his funeral. Even his own children didn't come. How sad that a man could achieve so much and yet be loved or valued by so few. Whether or not he fit Solomon's definition of a fool is not my call to make. But certainly that is the danger of living a life full of foolish choices. As Solomon states, "The lips of the righteous feed many: but fools die for want of wisdom" (Proverbs 10:21).

◉◉ The Signs of a Fool

Solomon teaches that if we act like a fool long enough, we are likely to become one. He offers us a number of attributes that reveal foolish behavior. I share these with the hope that if you recognize these in your life, you'll make whatever changes are needed to alter your behavior and thinking. I have made many foolish choices. And without the compass that Solomon provides, I, too, might have ended my life as one of Solomon's fools.

They close their ears to instruction. "YOU'RE telling ME how to read dialogue?" exclaimed a famous television actor as I was directing him in a television commercial. I was taken aback. Previously, I had directed such Academy Award winners as Charlton Heston, Mickey Rooney, Cher, and Jane Fonda— more than seventy movie and television stars—without encountering such resistance. I had produced hundreds of successful television campaigns, generating billions of dollars in sales. I had created and written this particular commercial. I knew how it needed to be read to be believable to consumers. And yet this celebrity refused to read it that way, and the project failed. Instead of making millions of dollars in royalties, as so many of our celebrity endorsers have, he made only a few thousand. His pride had blinded him; he made a foolish decision. In Proverbs 1:7, Solomon says, "But fools despise wisdom and instruction." There have been many times in my life when I, too, have refused instruction. Fortunately, Solomon's statement completely changed the way I view counsel from others. A wise man or woman *seeks out* and values any instruction they can receive in the important endeavors in their lives.

Fools tend to "shoot from the lip." They say whatever they think or feel without thorough consideration. In Proverbs 10:14, Solomon says, "The mouth of a fool invites ruin." Jobs are lost, careers are ruined, and marriages disintegrate because people say stupid things without pausing for reflection.

They repeat the same foolish behavior. Einstein once said that the definition of insanity was trying something that didn't work over and over again and expecting different results. Solomon said it this way: "As a dog returns to its vomit, so a fool repeats his folly."

They don't respond to punishment. In Proverbs 27:22, Solomon writes, "Though you grind a fool in a mortar, grinding him like grain with a pestle [hammer], you will not remove his folly from him." All of us make foolish decisions. When punished by authorities or by life, we usually change our errant ways. Not so with a fool. One of my former bosses (with a genius IQ) made millions of dollars in a fraudulent scheme. The FTC prosecuted, and he went to prison. He came out of prison and created a whole new fraudulent scheme in an entirely different industry. The FTC prosecuted, and he went to prison again. He came out of prison and started a new business, and once again was shut down by the FTC. That was fifteen years ago, and I lost track of him. A few days ago, I thought about him and did a Google search. His name came up as the driving force behind a recent national scandal in which thousands of women had been bilked out of their savings. He is being prosecuted once again. This man is undoubtedly one of the most brilliant men I have ever known, and yet, by Solomon's definition, he is a fool.

Fools trust solely in their own heart. "It *felt* so right" is often the reason people give for doing something that later turns out to have been wrong. We all make decisions based upon our emotions, on how we feel. Sometimes such choices work out. But a person who relies upon how he or she feels as the primary factor in their decision making is a fool, according to Solomon. He wrote, "He who trusts in his own heart is a fool." The fact is that our emotions are often blinded or hijacked by our misperceptions. We ignore or fail to seek the counsel of others; we fail to "look well into a matter," and act upon our feelings. Yes, we should take our feelings into consideration when we make a decision. But we should not base any decision solely upon our feelings. It's a sure way to crash and burn.

They tear down their own house. Our homes should be a safe harbor for us and our families. And yet for many, homes are anything but that. Instead, they are places filled with discouragement, criticism, contention, and sometimes physical, verbal, or emotional abuse. In Proverbs 14:1, Solomon says, "The wise woman builds her house, but the foolish tears it down with her own hands." Everyone wants loving and fulfilling relationships with their spouse and children. And yet they unwisely do so many things that tear each other down and ultimately bring about the dissolution of their marriage and the disintegration of their family. Whether through criticism, anger, or infidelity, fools tear down their houses with their own hands. Solomon contrasts that with a wise woman or man who does everything they can to encourage and love their family, building their home into the kind of safe harbor it was meant to be.

Fools Deny God. It's one thing to say you don't *know* whether God exists. That may be the honest statement of a man or woman who has not seen enough evidence to draw the conclusion that God exists. However, it's quite another thing to "believe in your heart" that God does *not* exist, and to then act out a life based on that belief. Solomon's father, King David, calls such a person a fool. In Psalm 14:1 he wrote, "The fool has said in his heart, 'There is no God'." Notice, David isn't singling out those who deny God with their words, but rather the person who has said in his *heart* "there is no God." The heart is the core of a person's feelings and beliefs. The person who truly believes there is no God will likely live a life with no heartfelt accountability to moral or ethical laws. David said in Psalm 14 that such a person will live a morally corrupt life and will do things that are abominable to God. Solomon would agree that those words accurately describe a fool.

◉◉ Solomon's Strategies for Acquiring Wisdom

How can we acquire the kind of wisdom Solomon talks about? Solomon gives us a handful of specific steps that we can take:

Search for wisdom as you would search for hidden treasure. Few treasures are lying in plain sight. They have to be actively searched for. Solomon tells us to pursue wisdom with the passion of a gold miner, and value it more than we would value gold and other treasures. Pay whatever cost it takes to acquire it, and once you have it, never disregard it. Value wisdom more than your wealth or any of your possessions. In our modern vernacular, he would say value wisdom and the strategies he reveals more than you value your bank account or investment portfolio.

SOLOMON'S FOUNDATION FOR SUCCESS 239

Listen. Remain a learner your whole life. Go into every situation asking questions instead of giving answers. In Proverbs 1:5, Solomon says, "A wise man will hear and increase in learning, and a man of understanding will acquire wise counsel." Wisdom does not come from within. Wisdom comes from sources outside of ourselves. Remember the benefits of seeking counsel.

In Proverbs 1:8, Solomon gives one more piece of advice: "Hear the instruction of your father and forsake not the law of your mother." Now, this is more than a platitude. When I was a teenager, my father and I argued for days about whether or not I would take a typing class in high school. I told him typing was for girls and I would be embarrassed to take the class. He told me that he had always been frustrated because he couldn't type, and he insisted that I take it for a year. Finally, we reached a compromise. I would take typing for one semester. If, at the end of the semester, I was the fastest typist in the class, I would not have to take it for a second semester. If I was not, I would have to take it for a second semester. As it turned out, I had to take typing for only one semester. But that single semester of typing changed my entire life. Before I learned how to type, I could not write fast enough to keep up with my thoughts, and even if I did, nobody could read my writing (including me). And when I slowed down to write more neatly, I would lose my train of thought. Typing changed everything. I could literally type my thoughts as fast as they came into my mind. As it turned out, my entire career has revolved around my typing. During the past thirty years, I have written hundreds of commercials and shows. My writing has produced hundreds of millions of dollars in income for my partners and me. On top of that, I've had the joy of writing a number of bestselling books that I believe have helped people achieve more success and fulfillment in their lives. Had I not followed my father's advice to learn how to type, I would not have written even *one* television script or book. Even as adults, we should carefully consider our parents' advice. No one loves us more and is more concerned for our well-being.

Study the Book of Proverbs. In Proverbs 4:20–22, Solomon writes, "My son, give attention to my words; Incline your ear to my sayings. Do not let them depart from your sight; Keep them in the midst of your heart. For they are life to those who find them, and health to all their whole body." Solomon truly believed that the wisdom he had articulated in the Book of Proverbs did not originate in his mind, but rather had been given to him by God. The Proverbs I have referred to in this book comprise less than one-fifth of the total number contained in the Book of Proverbs. The wisdom they contain is truly incomparable. I urge you to follow Solomon's advice and study his words.

Receive. You will never receive any of the life-giving benefits of water or food by merely tasting them. The same is true with wisdom. Simply becoming aware of knowledge and understanding will do little to increase the worth of your life. In Proverbs 4:10, Solomon says, "Hear oh my son and *receive* my saying." For understanding to be transformed into wisdom, we must receive it and let it change who we are. By receiving or accepting it into our heart, it will manifest itself in our attitudes and behavior.

Apply Your **Heart** *to Understanding.* In Proverbs 2:2 Solomon says, "Make your ear attentive to wisdom, incline your heart to understanding." In other words, pay attention to wisdom and make it a part of who you are; right to the very core of your personality. Follow wisdom's leading with your *whole* heart. Make its precepts part of your daily life. In Proverbs 4:23 (NIV) we are told, "Above all else, guard your heart, for it is the wellspring of life." Solomon would have you expose your heart first and foremost to wisdom, while you erect a wall between your heart and foolishness. Getting wisdom into your heart will result in wise attitudes and behavior flowing out of your heart to bless your own life and the lives of those you influence.

Keep the precepts of wisdom at the front of your thoughts and vision. Thirty-two years ago Gary Smalley challenged me to read a chapter of Proverbs every day for two years. The results were miraculous.

Solomon urges you to do the same thing that Gary asked me to do. In Proverbs 3:21–24, he writes, "My son, preserve sound judgment and discernment, do not let them out of your sight; they will be life for you, an ornament to grace your neck. Then you will go on your way in safety, and your foot will not stumble; when you lie down, you will not be afraid; when you lie down, your sleep will be sweet." "Hold on to instruction," he writes later, "do not let it go; guard it well, for it is your life."

Honor God as the God of the Universe and the God of Your Life. Although this is the last step I will discuss in this chapter, it was Solomon's *first* step to acquiring wisdom. And he plainly states that for all of us, this is the first step to building a foundation of wisdom. In Proverbs 1:7 he writes, "The fear of the Lord is the beginning of knowledge." And in Proverbs 9:10 he says, "The fear of the Lord is the beginning of wisdom." When Solomon talks about "fearing the Lord" he's not talking about being *terrified* by God. Instead, he's talking about holding God in the highest esteem; honoring and valuing Him as the God of the universe and crowning Him the Lord—or reigning King—of your life.

Why does Solomon say that fearing God is the *beginning* of wisdom? The answer is simple: From Solomon's perspective, if God exists then by definition anything God says is the ultimate truth by which all else must be measured. Wisdom is the knowledge, understanding, and application of truth; not half-truths but whole truths. If God has spoken, then his words are the navigational instruments upon which we must rely throughout our journey through life. Without those instruments we will drift off course and end in a terrible crash. That's why Solomon could give us such an incredible contrast in three verses from his book of Proverbs. On one hand he tells us in Proverbs 28:26, "He who trusts in his own heart is a fool." On the other hand, he tells us in Proverbs 3:5-6 (NKJV), "Trust in the Lord with all your heart, and lean not on your own understanding; in all your ways acknowledge Him, and He shall direct your paths."

Who in the universe could possess more wisdom than God? And who in the universe could serve as a more reliable guide? Solomon tells us that if we trust in God with all of our heart, and search out His will in all of our ways, then He will direct the course of our life. That is the most wonderful promise Solomon makes in all of his Proverbs.

It is important to understand that Solomon is *not* talking about trusting a church, a religious tradition, or a Christian leader. He's talking about a trust-based relationship with God. The wisdom contained in the Proverbs provides you with incomparable direction to achieve success and fulfillment, both personally and professionally. But only a trust-based relationship with God can fill the vacuum in your heart and bring eternal purpose to your life. To help you in this endeavor, I would urge you to read one of the best books I have ever read on this subject, *The Purpose Driven Life,* by pastor Rick Warren. May God richly bless your pursuit of wisdom and your relationship with Him.

Knowledge to Wisdom
TURNING PRECEPTS INTO ACTION

1. Read the Book of Proverbs, a chapter a day. Have a pen and paper handy to write down the insights you gain and how to apply them to your life that day. I have divided the wisdom in the Book of Proverbs into forty-six categories. In this book, I have touched upon only fifteen of those categories. Think of the incredible insights that await you.

2. In your study of the Book of Proverbs, I would highly recommend using a modern translation. Often, the seventeenth-century King James Version is difficult to follow. In this book, I have quoted most often from the New American Standard Bible (NASB) and the New International Version (NIV).

3. The single greatest flaw of most books is that even though they give the reader wonderful ideas and values, they do not teach the specific skills necessary to apply those ideas and values to a daily routine. I have prepared material to help readers learn specific skills to apply Solomon's laws of life to their own daily lives. You are welcome to look at these books, journals, and workbooks at my Web site: stevenkscott.com. I highly recommend my previous book, *Mentored by a Millionaire—The Master Strategies of Super Achievers,* not because I wrote it but because it teaches every skill necessary to bring not only those strategies into your life, but the precepts of Solomon, as well. In terms of relationships, I recommend two of Gary Smalley's books, *The DNA of Relationships* and *Making Love Last Forever.*

—— ◎◎ ——

CHAPTER 16

Partnering With the Ultimate Mentor

Trust in the Lord with all your heart, and lean not on your
own understanding; in all your ways acknowledge Him,
and He shall direct your paths.

PROVERBS 3:5-6 (NKJV)

My whole life changed when I found a mentor and a group of
partners. Prior to that, I had flunked out of my first nine jobs
in my first six years after college. Then, following Solomon's
advice, I partnered with my mentor and a few other partners,
and together we were able to create more than two dozen
multi-million dollar businesses. That was the power of find-
ing a mentor and partners.

Now imagine for a moment that *you* are going to start a new
business, but unfortunately you're broke. How would you
like to have the following seven partners who would be totally
committed to you and your new business? Warren Buffet, the
most savvy investor in the world, would be your *financial* partner; George W. Bush would be your political partner; Donald
Trump would be your real estate partner; the Walton family
and the Nordstrom family would be your retailing partners;

Steven Spielberg would be your media partner; and the Mayo Clinic would be your partner for all your health issues. Would that be a powerful partnership or what? Warren Buffet, George W. Bush, Donald Trump, Sam Walton's family, the Nordstrom family, Steven Spielberg, and the Mayo Clinic. What a partnership!

Well Solomon found one partner and mentor who was greater than all of these partners *combined*. Solomon's partner owned all the world's wealth and was more powerful than earthquakes and hurricanes. His partner could see the future in clear detail, and could change the course of events. His partner could move the hearts and minds of men and women. His partner even had power over life and death. Can you believe that Solomon, in the early years of his adult life, was able to hook up with such a mentor? From that partnership, Solomon received more wealth and wisdom than any man who has ever lived. And here's the best news you'll ever hear: His partner is alive and well today, and wants to be *your* partner and mentor as well.

If you believe that God is still active in the affairs of mankind you're going to really like this chapter because you're going to gain Solomon's wisdom and strategies for the most incredible partnering and mentoring relationship you'll ever experience. If, however, you get a little nervous when there is too much religious talk connected with your business or financial dealings, then you can close this book now to avoid any potential discomfort. But at least do yourself the favor of considering this: Although a mentoring and partnering relationship with God may be nothing more than an *option* for you, it was non-optional for Solomon at the beginning of his reign as the king of Israel. And look how he prospered as a result.

◎◎ Solomon's Two Greatest Concepts

Of all of the insights, principles, strategies, and laws of life proclaimed by Solomon, two stand above all others. The first is his concept of *fearing the Lord*. When Solomon talks about "fearing" the Lord he's not talking about being terrified of God, but rather he's talking about holding God in the highest esteem; honoring and valuing Him as the God of the universe, and crowning Him as the Lord and reigning boss of your life. That means learning to love what God loves and turning away from that which He is against. Solomon's second essential concept is the means by which we can have a trust-based *personal and intimate relationship* with God. Interestingly, to lay claim to a trust-based relationship with God, you must first begin to hold Him in the highest esteem. You cannot trust in a God you do not know. And the God Solomon knew and proclaimed in the Proverbs is a God who is so awesome that to truly know Him you must honor and value Him for *all* that He is. Out of that awareness, honor, and value will come the foundation upon which your trust can be established.

FEAR OF THE LORD: Holding the God of Abraham in the highest esteem, and honoring and valuing Him as the God of the universe (the *only* God) and crowning Him as the Lord and reigning boss of your life, day by day.

The reason I say these are the two greatest concepts ever proclaimed by Solomon is because applying them to your life brings the greatest rewards Solomon describes in the Book of Proverbs. Here are the rewards that Solomon says we can expect when we *truly* hold God in awe and crown Him as the reigning boss of our daily life.

True knowledge and wisdom. In Proverbs 1:7 and 9:10, we're told that the fear of the Lord is the *beginning* of understanding and wisdom. Why is this the foundation of wisdom? Because God knows everything. He alone knows the ultimate truth by which all other information must be measured. He alone knows what possesses true value and what does not. So when you fear God, honor Him, hold Him in awe, and make Him the boss of your daily life, *then* He can communicate to you that which is right and that which has true and lasting value. Then you will gain wisdom as you apply to your life those things that are right in God's eyes and which possess lasting value.

Happiness that lasts. Proverbs 28:14 states, "How blessed is the man who fears always." On the surface, this statement appears to be an oxymoron; after all, how can you

be happy if you are living in fear? However, there is no con-
tradiction when you realize that Solomon is not talking about
earthly anxiety or terror, but his concept of fearing the Lord.
Understanding this, we could paraphrase Solomon's statement with these words: "Happy is the man who grants the
highest esteem to God alone and honors Him as the God of
the universe, and crowns him daily as the king of his life."
The word Solomon uses for happiness isn't synonymous with
cheerfulness, but rather is more akin to a deep and abiding
inner joy that no one can take away from you.

Strong confidence. In Proverbs 14:26 Solomon says, "In
the fear of the Lord there is strong confidence." True confidence is *not* something you gain by psyching yourself up. We
gain confidence not from within, but from fearing God. And
who doesn't want confidence? It is a wonderful commodity
because it pushes worry out of our mind and heart. We have
all failed so many times that any confidence we have in ourselves is easily shaken. We find it much easier to place our
confidence in others who have a history of not letting us
down. For example, we are so confident in the abilities of
commercial airline pilots that we let them transport us at
35,000 feet at nearly six hundred miles per hour. We're so
confident in the stability and trustworthiness of financial
institutions that we let them hold our life savings.

We can have a similarly high level of confidence in our
own activities *when* we know that our paths are being guided
by the most powerful and wisest being in the universe. God
promises to direct the paths of those who trust in Him with

all of their hearts and who acknowledge Him in all their ways (see Proverbs 3:5-6). In Proverbs 16:9 Solomon states, "The mind of man plans his way, but the Lord directs his steps." If I fear the Lord, I will trust Him with all my heart and acknowledge him in all my ways. As I do that, I will have the confidence that *He* is directing my paths. Even if that path takes me through heartache and suffering I will have the confidence that *He* is leading me into the center of His master plan. This bedrock confidence is promised only to those who truly fear the Lord.

A safe place to hide and rest. How often does your life get so crazy that you just want to check out for awhile? It happens to all of us. At times, you just want to get away and be by yourself. You want to find a hotel room or an isolated place in the mountains or just about any place where you an hide and rest. Or have you ever been in a fearful situation that caused you to wish for a safe place to hide? In Proverbs 14:26, Solomon tells us that people who fear the Lord will have a safe place of refuge, even for their children.

The avoidance of deadly traps. In Proverbs 14:27 (KJV) Solomon tells us, "The fear of the Lord is a fountain of life, to depart from the snares of death." In the previous chapter we saw in Proverbs 16:25 (NKJV) that "There is a way that seems right to a man, but its end is the way of death." When you fear the Lord, you are assured that He will provide you with a fountain of life that will lead you *away* from traps that can bring about your spiritual demise and even your physical death. Does that mean that fearing God protects us against death? Of course not. It simply means that we will not be entrapped by anything that can bring about our spiritual death or our physical death outside of God's perfect timing.

Satisfaction and fulfillment. In Proverbs 19:23 (NKJV) we're told: "The fear of the Lord leads to life, and he who has it will abide in satisfaction; he will not be visited with evil." The world is full of people who are not satisfied or fulfilled. According to one recent survey, eighty percent of all adults wished they could find a more satisfying job. The fact that fifty percent of all marriages end in divorce tells us that at least half the marriages don't provide the satisfaction and fulfillment the couple was hoping for. How about you? How would you rate your level of satisfaction, purpose, and fulfillment—at home and at work?

According to Solomon, the way to gain more satisfaction is not necessarily to look for a new job, but rather to become an apprentice to the God of the universe. Begin to hold Him in the highest esteem, honor Him as God, and make Him the boss of your daily life. Do this, and you will experience a level of satisfaction and fulfillment that you have never known before. At the same time you will be slamming shut the door of your heart and mind to evil influences that would hijack your spirit. That's the promise of this proverb to those who truly fear the Lord.

Riches, honor, and life. Solomon's statement in Proverbs 22:4 surprised me the first time I read it. "The reward of humility and the fear of the Lord are riches, honor and life." I could understand how a person who is truly humble and fears the Lord would attain honor with others and a more purposeful and fulfilling life. But what about riches? The Hebrew word that Solomon uses in this Proverb does mean *material* riches. So at first I wondered: Is he actually promising material wealth to the person who is humble and fears the Lord? Then I realized this Proverb is not necessarily presented as a promise or a law of life. It is more likely a statement of what Solomon had observed.

The people Solomon knew who feared the Lord and were humble had by and large attained honor, a fulfilling life, and a degree of material wealth that surpassed the economic norms of the day. Likewise, people today who are humble and fear the Lord will attain honor with others, a more purpose-filled life, and a level of material wealth that exceeds the *norms* of their respective culture. In a Third World country where the population is facing starvation, simply having food, clothing, and adequate shelter would qualify a person as rich by comparison. A person who truly fears the Lord acquires wisdom and understanding. And applying wisdom and understanding to commerce can easily move a person up the economic ladder.

Jesus, on the other hand, talked about two kinds of riches. He talked about riches on earth that can be stolen or suffer decay, and riches in heaven that last for eternity. He told us to keep our focus on the latter and to order our lives in a way that will enable us to store up those eternal treasures. These *greater* riches are the ultimate reward for those who are humble and fear the Lord. Jesus asks in Mark 8:36 (KJV): "What shall it profit a man, if he shall gain the whole world, and lose his own soul?"

Prolonged life. In Proverbs 10:27 (KJV), we are told that "the fear of the Lord prolongs days." That is, it makes your days on earth more fulfilling and it gives you more days of life. My twelve-year old son recently told me that he wanted me to live until I was ninety-four. He then told me how old he and each of his brothers and sisters would be when I died. He figured my youngest daughter would be forty-two and he would be fifty. He told me, "It might be a little harder on Hallie, but I'll help her through it." Knowing that I need to live another thirty-eight years to hit that mark, this Proverb is especially important to me and my children. Although I know that every day of life is a gift from the Lord and that He owes me nothing, this Proverb is still music to my ears.

๑๏ The Consequences of *Not* Having a Trust-Based Relationship With God

You won't do yourself any favors if you assume that ignorance is bliss and remain unaware of Solomon's wisdom. Not knowing the ultimate truth about the things that are most important can result in tremendous losses. If God exists then it makes sense that there are absolute truths that set the standard by which every human will either be judged or shown mercy. Don't wait until you are dead before you find out what these truths are.

Imagine if you went to sleep and then woke up face-to-face with God. How terrible it would be to discover that you could have had a far more purposeful and joyful lifetime had you only experienced a personal relationship with God; a relationship that had been available to you all along. To discover that your life had been wasted in relation to God and eternity would certainly qualify as a catastrophe. Even more terrible would be the discovery that you would spend eternity separated from God, when you could have enjoyed eternity *with* Him. Solomon lists a number of specific consequences that overcome those who go through life without a personal, trust-based relationship with God. Here are just four of them.

A life characterized by foolishness. "Wait a minute," you say, "I know a lot of brilliant people who don't have the kind of relationship with God that Solomon talks about. How could you call these people foolish?" No matter how brilliant a person may be, *if* he misses out on the most important aspect of life, how *wise* can he be? If he enjoys a lifetime of success and wealth but in the end experiences an eternity of despair and torment, how wise is he? Even in life, the most brilliant person who does not experience a personal relationship with God will make wrong choices resulting in life-altering mistakes. In Proverbs 1:7, Solomon writes: "The fear of the Lord is the beginning of knowledge; fools despise wisdom and instruction." That is, they despise wisdom and instruction as it relates to that which matters most, namely pleasing God.

Getting into trouble. In Proverbs 28:14 (NIV), Solomon says: "Blessed is the man who always fears the Lord, but he who hardens his heart falls into trouble." This Proverb reveals two incredible truths. First, it makes clear that hardening your heart is the opposite of fearing the Lord. This implies that everyone feels their conscience drawing them toward a personal relationship with God. To resist that inclination, they ignore it, fight it, and finally harden their heart to it. That is when they begin to fall into trouble. It can be personal trouble, business trouble, career trouble, marital trouble, and nearly always moral trouble. This is what happened to Solomon when his arrogance began to suppress and supplant his fear of the Lord and his trust-based relationship with God. I too have fallen into trouble when my arrogance replaced my fear of the Lord. There was a time when I began to pay less attention to God and His word. I didn't honor Him as God, but rather went my own way as if He didn't exist. In my arrogance I hurt my wife, my children, and everyone else who loved me.

A shortened life. In a day when society focuses on ways to extend life, Solomon tells us that failing to fear the Lord will shorten one's life. In Proverbs 10:27 (NKJV), he says: "The fear of the LORD prolongs days, but the years of the wicked will be shortened." Trouble creates stress, and medical science has proven that stress shortens a person's life. It increases rates of heart disease, cancer, and other life-threatening conditions. On top of that, people in trouble tend to pay less attention to rules and laws that exist to protect them. For example, they may think speed limits or laws against drinking and driving apply only to others. Typically, the lower a person's ethics, the more likely it is that he will live a lifestyle that includes significant health risks.

Loss of all the benefits of fearing God. One of the greatest consequences of not fearing God is losing the benefits that you would have otherwise enjoyed from a trust-based relationship with Him. For example, you could go through life without understanding the true purpose of your life. You have no secure place to hide and rest. You become susceptible to life's traps that lead to death. You go through life without a shield of protection from evil people. You live without the confidence that comes from knowing you are doing what is right and best, and without the confidence that your paths are being made level and straight by the God of the universe.

◎◎ Fearing God and Experiencing a Trust-Based Relationship with Him

What does it take to experience the kind of relationship with God that Solomon wrote about? As Solomon demonstrates, it involves much more than a one-time prayer of repentance and commitment. Fearing God and experiencing a trust-based relationship only *begins* with a prayer. It continues by choosing to trust God and valuing Him as the God of your life moment-by-moment.

In John 17:3 (NKJV) Jesus said, "And this is eternal life, that they may know You, the only true God, and Jesus Christ whom You have sent." Eternal life is wholly contained in intimately knowing God the Father and His Son, the Lord Jesus

Christ. Jeremiah 9:23-24 (NKJV) says, "Thus says the Lord: 'Let not the wise man glory in his wisdom, let not the mighty man glory in his might, nor let the rich man glory in his riches; but let him who glories glory in this, *that he understands and knows Me,* that I am the Lord, exercising lovingkindness, judgment, and righteousness in the earth, for in these I delight,' says the Lord." The Greek verb translated "know" in John 17, and the Hebrew verb translated "know" in Jeremiah, are synonymous with the word *intimacy.* What God wants with you and me is an intimate love-trust relationship.

Getting to Know God—Intimately

There's nothing magical or mystical to getting to know God in the way He desires to be known. Fortunately for us, He has revealed Himself in both the written Word of God (the Bible) and in the living Word of God (the person of Jesus of Nazareth). There is however one seemingly insurmountable barrier that stands between God and us. It's a barrier that cannot be climbed over, flown over, or circumvented in any way. That barrier is our sin. God is perfect and holy in every way. We, on the other hand, have all sinned. Romans 3:23 says: "For all have sinned and fall short of the glory of God." Even worse, Romans 6:23 tells us: "For the wages of sin is death…." Our sin has created an irreconcilable difference between us and God. And our sin has *earned* us a terrible wage—spiritual death and eternal separation from God.

However, God has provided a way for us to be reconciled to him so that we can enjoy an intimate relationship with Him that will replace our earned-wage of death. God offers us a free gift, a gift greater than any other, the gift of eternal life. He offers us this gift through the person of His Son, Jesus Christ. Jesus came to earth, lived a perfect, sinless life, and then took our sins upon Himself and received the judgment that we deserve to suffer. And here's the best news of all: His atoning sacrifice on the cross was not a partial payment for our sin; nor was it merely a down payment for our eternal life to be followed by additional payments from us. It was the *full* payment of our debt to God. Moments before He died on the cross, Jesus said, "it is finished" (John 19:30, KJV). He didn't mean his life was finished, but rather that everything that had to be done to pay for our sins had been done, once and for all. The Greek phrase he uttered was the same phrase that was written on certificates of debt when they were paid off. It literally means "paid in full."

When you pay off a mortgage or car loan and the banker cancels your debt, how many more payments must you then make? None! Jesus' death on the cross paid the penalty for all of our sins, in full. However, there's only one way to apply that payment to our personal debt. According to the New Testament, we must believe in Jesus and receive Him as our Lord and Savior. Jesus said, "For God so loved the world that He gave His only begotten Son; that whoever believes in Him shall not perish but have everlasting life" (John 3:16). In John 1:11-12 (KJV) we're told: "He came unto His own, and His own received Him not; but as many as received Him, to them gave He power to become the sons of God, even to them that believe on his name."

In John 5:23 (NKJV) Jesus said: "He who does not honor the Son does not honor the Father who sent him." In other words, it is impossible to fear God in the way that Solomon talks about if you do not fully embrace and honor His only begotten Son. And the *only* way to honor the Son is to make Him the Lord of your life. *He* is the key to having the type of relationship with God that Solomon and his father, David, wrote about. That's why Jesus could say in John 14:6 (KJV): "I am the way, the truth, and the life: no man cometh unto the Father, but by me."

So the question at hand is "how?" How can we come to know God intimately through His Son? First, we must place our faith in the person of Jesus Christ and believe that He received the full punishment for our sins when He was crucified on our behalf. Second, we must believe that God the Father accepted Jesus' payment for our sins; and that Jesus was resurrected from the dead and is alive today. Third, as evidence of that faith we must change the direction of our lives. Instead of continuing to be the god of our own lives, we must choose to make Jesus Christ the reigning Lord of our daily lives, letting His word and the Holy Spirit guide and direct our behavior. Our number-one priority in life must become getting to know Him. After we have chosen to make Him the Lord of our lives, we can get to know Him in an intimate way through two-way communication. We communicate with Him through prayer, and He communicates with us through the Bible, His written word. The Apostle Paul gave us tremendous insights in both of these areas, but I will only briefly touch upon two of them.

In Romans 10:17 (NKJV) Paul wrote: "Faith comes by hearing, and hearing by the word of God." As we study God's word, our faith will be established and built up. David wrote: "Thy word have I hid in mine heart that I might not sin against thee" (Psalm 119:11, KJV). God has spoken to us and revealed His will for us in the Old and New Testaments of the Bible. Reading and meditating upon His word is the *only* way our faith can be built up.

In 1 Thessalonians 5:17, Paul instructed us to "pray without ceasing." This doesn't mean you bow down on your knees all your waking hours, but rather that you constantly converse with God throughout your day. The Bible gives us dozens of insights and promises regarding prayer, but Paul reveals the essence and cornerstone of prayer in Philippians 4:6-7. "Be anxious for nothing, but in everything by prayer and supplication with thanksgiving let your requests be made known to God. And the peace of God, which surpasses all comprehension, will guard your hearts and your minds in Christ Jesus."

Paul is telling us to talk to God about everything that is on our mind. We're told to not hold *anything* back, but rather tell Him exactly what we are thinking and feeling, and don't worry about how He will receive it. We're told to tell him exactly what we want, and to do that with a grateful heart. Why should we be grateful when we're praying, even before God answers our prayers? Because He has chosen to listen to us and has given us an opportunity to communicate with

Him. How grateful would you be if the President of the United States invited you to the Oval Office, specifically so that he could listen to everything that's on your mind? If you would be grateful for that, how much more grateful should you be to enter into the presence of the God of the universe, to tell Him everything that's on your mind?

Paul says that when we pray in this manner, then the peace of God will actively guard our hearts and minds (see Philippians 4:7). This is a supreme peace, a peace so great that it exceeds our comprehension. As God has the freedom to reveal Himself, His Son, and His Spirit to you through His words in the Bible; and as you freely and *honestly* reveal yourself to Him through prayer, intimacy will follow.

As our faith grows from reading God's word and our intimacy with Him grows through our two-way communication, then the trust-based relationship that Solomon talks about becomes a reality. The good news is we can start making that a reality right now, simply by doing what Solomon directs us to do in Proverbs 3:5-6. As we make the choice to trust God and follow His word in each choice we face, then He *will* direct our paths. "Trust in the Lord with all your heart and do not lean on your own understanding. In all your ways acknowledge Him, and He will make your paths straight." God *wants* to be our trusted partner and mentor.

Three More Ways to Honor God

As we have seen, it is impossible to honor God without embracing Jesus Christ as our Savior and the reigning Lord of

262 THE RICHEST MAN WHO EVER LIVED

our lives. That is the first step in honoring God, and honoring God is the essence of *fearing* God. We also honor Him by building a trust-based relationship with Him. But Solomon doesn't stop there. He reveals three other important ways that we are to honor God.

Choose to do that which is right and to* not *do the things we know to be wrong. In Proverbs 14:2 (NKJV), Solomon writes: "He who walks in his uprightness fears the LORD, but he who is perverse in his ways despises Him." Do you love God or despise Him? Solomon says that loving or despising God has nothing to do with how you feel, but it has everything to do with how you act. By choosing to do what is right you honor God with your life; and when you choose to act unrighteously, or choose perversion over righteousness, *that* is despising or hating God. God wants us to honor our partnership with Him, approaching Him in awe and ordering our behavior according to His laws, wisdom, and teachings.

Choose to hate what God hates. Yes, God actually does *hate* some things. In Proverbs 8:13, Solomon says: "The fear of the LORD is to hate evil; pride and arrogance and the evil way...I hate." Wow. God hates pride, arrogance, evil, and evil ways! Today more than any time in church history, men and women are trying to experience the benefits of a personal relationship with God while they continue to embrace the things God hates. Jesus said, "These people honor me with their lips, but their hearts are far from me" (Matthew 15:8, NIV). He also said: "No man can serve two masters: for either he will hate the one, and love the other; or else he will hold to the one, and despise the other" (Matthew 6:24, KJV). Today, men and women want everything God has to offer while they choose to serve other masters; masters such as self-centeredness, materialism, adultery, and perversions of all kinds.

You cannot honor and embrace God when you love what He hates. You must choose your master, every day, dozens or even hundreds of times a day. Perhaps the gravest warning in all of Scripture is found in Mathew 7:22-23. Jesus foretold the great judgment with these words: "Many will say to Me on that day, 'Lord, Lord, did we not prophesy in Your name, and in Your name cast out demons, and in Your name perform many miracles?' And then I will declare to them, 'I never knew you; depart from Me, you who practice lawlessness'." Jesus isn't talking about leading a sinless life. He's talking about choosing to live a life that follows Him down paths of righteous behavior, and daily repenting for unrighteous attitudes, thoughts, words, and deeds. Rather than rationalizing, denying, or excusing our sins, He wants us to acknowledge them as wrong and see them from His point of view. In 1 John 1:6-7 we're told: "If we say that we have fellowship with Him and yet walk in the darkness, we lie and do not practice the truth; but if we walk in the Light as He Himself is in the Light, we have fellowship with one another, and the blood of Jesus His Son cleanses us from all sin." And in 1 John 1:9 we're told, "If we confess our sins, He is faithful and righteous to forgive us our sins, and to cleanse us from all unrighteousness."

Stop being a know-it-all and walk away from evil. In

Proverbs 3:7 Solomon states: "Do not be wise in your own eyes; Fear the Lord and turn away from evil." We honor God when we exchange our ignorance for His wisdom and depart from the wrong practices and paths of our lives. We literally change directions, turning our back to the evil ways of our past so we can turn our face toward God and His righteous ways.

✆ When We Fear God, We Gain the Greatest Treasure in The Universe

Who wouldn't want to learn how to take possession of the world's greatest treasure? In Proverbs 15:16 Solomon writes: "Better is a little with the fear of the LORD than great treasure and turmoil with it." There is no greater treasure than having an eternal, intimate relationship with the God of the universe, a God who loves you so much that He sent His only begotten Son to bear all of the terrible judgment for your sin. Solomon knew that no other treasure in this life could compare to such a treasure as this. While all other treasures are left behind at death, this one is not! It's the one treasure you can take with you into eternity. Honoring God the way He desires to be honored, through a personal relationship with the Lord Jesus Christ, produces what Jesus referred to as "treasures in heaven" (Matthew 6:20, KJV). These are treasures that cannot be stolen, destroyed, or tarnished by time. My prayer for you is that you will enter into the wonderful relationship that God has made available to you through the Lord Jesus Christ. In Revelation 3:20, Jesus makes the most wonderful invitation and promise ever made. He says: "Behold, I stand at the door and knock. If any man hears my voice and opens the door, I will come in to him, and dine with him and he with me."

Jesus invites you to enter into a personal relationship and day-by-day fellowship with Him that will last for eternity. I pray that you will take Him up on His offer. The heavenly treasures that you will inherit will make *you* the richest man or woman who ever lived.

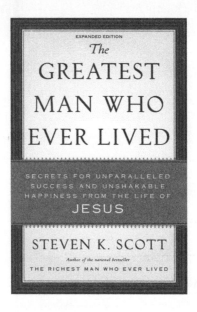

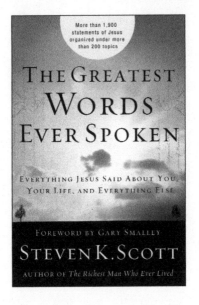

ABOUT THE AUTHOR

STEVEN K. SCOTT, a writer, producer, director, and marketing entrepreneur, is the cofounder of American Telecast Corporation. Along with his partners, he has created more than a dozen businesses that have achieved billions of dollars in sales. He has authored five international bestsellers and is a popular national speaker on the subject of personal and professional achievement.

www.stevenkscott.com
www.waterbrookpress.com